Praise for Phillip Pooped in my Pink Patent Leather Purse

"Have gotten up to chapter 2 and haven't stopped crying yet!! Absolutely fantastic and amazing!"

—Patricia Zell, mother of Wendy Zell

"Wow. I read your memoir in one sitting—stayed up last night taking it all in. This book radiates simplicity, joy, and inner strength. It makes us question why we make the choices we do while determining the core of our character when we hit rock bottom and have to rebuild. You have always been a beacon of strength…and after seeing the whole picture, this is wholeheartedly confirmed. Being true, honest, and raw about our own humanity is a gift, not easily obtained or owned. I admire every word, every detail, and every story. They are all proof that you are REAL (like the Velveteen Rabbit) and only confirm what I have seen and known in you all along. There are so many points that radiate from your work."

—With much love, Sydnie Canterberry

"Wendy, Thank you so much for sharing your memoir with me. I cannot even begin to tell you what a great read it was for me. I started it yesterday and stayed up until I finished it. I admire the courage, strength, and hard work you put into your writing. Reading about the crap you endured in life thus far was relatable to me. I'm trying to recover and restore my faith in humanity and forgive but not forget the unkind people in my own life. People suck!!! Anyways I loved it and I cannot wait to read your next book. You are one of a kind and I have always had a special place in my heart for you! You were an important part of shaping, teaching, and advocating for Justin and helped him become a good student and I am forever grateful to you."

—Love, Brenda Tallent

"Wendy needed her memoir edited, and not only was it was a fantastic read, but she was also great to work with. Looking forward to working with her again soon!"

—Matt Cubberly, Editor of
Phillip Pooped in my Pink Patent Leather Purse

"Finished it!!!!! It was great! I can relate to so many things you've been through. Once I started reading I couldn't put it down. Relating to more and more in the book makes you want to keep reading. Trust me, more people can relate than you know. Keep on writing!!"

—Kim Lacey, childhood friend of Wendy and Todd

"I can tell already…it's very brave. And honest. The description of Mick broke my heart. Your writing was perfection. Made me cry. Well done, xoxo."

—Amy Lagae

Phillip Pooped in my Pink Patent Leather Purse

Also by Wendy Zell

Say Something Sunshine
(Coming Soon)

Phillip Pooped
in my
Pink Patent Leather Purse

*A Memoir
of*
Adversity,
Courage,
&
Self-Love

Wendy Zell

UNICORN
publications

Copyright © 2021 by Wendy Zell
All rights reserved.
Published by Unicorn Publications

No part of this book may be reproduced in any manner without written permission except in the case of brief quotations embodied in critical articles and reviews.

Although the author and publisher have made every effort to ensure that the information in this book was correct at press time, the author and publisher do not assume and hereby disclaim any liability to any party for any loss, damage, or disruption caused by errors or omissions, whether such errors or omissions result from negligence, accident, or any other cause. Forms and agreements are included for your information only.

For information about special discounts for bulk purchases or author interviews, appearances, and speaking engagements please contact:

Web: www.WendyZell.com
Facebook: www.facebook.com/ppimpplp
Instagram: @wendyzellauthor/
Email: wendyazell@gmail.com

First Edition

Edited by Matt Cubberly
All images © the Author unless noted
Cover, jacket, book design by Rodney Miles

For my Mom,
who inspires me to be
courageous and authentic.
I'm sorry for all the crap
I put you through
when I was younger.

For my Son,
because I love you
and hope you will
never give up on your dreams.
Anything is possible.

Contents

Prologue ix

A Little About Me xxii

Chapter 1: The Early Crap 1

Chapter 2: If I Was a Bird 9

Chapter 3: Poop Happens 15

Chapter 4: Unlucky 13 Crap 23

Chapter 5: It's About to Go Down 31

Chapter 6: Hot Shit! 39

Chapter 7: "If you're a really mean person, you're going to come back as a fly and eat poop." -Kurt Cobain 47

Chapter 8: Have a Nice Poop! 65

Chapter 9: Fancy Shit 73

Chapter 10: Flush it down… 83

Chapter 11: I Just Can't Get Away from this Shit! 89

Chapter 12: Holy Crap! 95

Chapter 13: "You don't have to poop! You're going to have a baby!" 105

Chapter 14: Deja Poo 113

Afterword 119

Epilogue.. 131
Acknowledgements 136
About the Author... 138

Prologue

BEFORE YOU BEGIN reading about all of the crap I've experienced in my life, let me take the opportunity to tell you about some of my blessings and accomplishments. I was born into a family of educators. My mother and father were both teachers when I was young. They met at Florida Atlantic University in Boca Raton during their college years. I have an older brother, John, who's two years older than me. I was born in Miami, Florida on Halloween, 1971. I loved my grandparents very much and enjoyed spending time with them until they passed on when I was in my late teens and twenties. I grew up in the sunny Florida playgrounds of the Atlantic Ocean and the Everglades, where I learned to appreciate nature and our vast oceans.

My family in Florida

Fort Lauderdale, Florida

My mother taught elementary school for twelve years, then continued her education and obtained her Master's Degree in Computer Science. Soon after, she pursued a career in administration and became an assistant principal for a decade, then principal for another ten years. I looked up to her in many ways over the years, because she was my first teacher. My mother was and still is very creative, intelligent, and thoughtful. She always threw the best parties and social functions, as everything was well thought out and purposefully special. She taught me how to cook, do laundry, and clean the house by age twelve. My mother loves clothes, jewelry, gemstones, travel, and fine things. It certainly wasn't easy meeting her high expectations of me, but I tried my best - even if I messed up a few times. I know that my Mom did the best she could to raise my brother and me to become strong-minded people.

Believe it or not, my father was who I wanted to stay home with me when I was sick, or when I just wanted to talk about life during my youth. He seemed to have great advice when I needed it most. My dad had a difficult childhood dealing with parent alcoholism and often being sick with asthma while he grew up in the windy city of Chicago. He's funny, talkative, and a great storyteller. My father was a special-education teacher for over thirty years in Miami and the Florida Keys. He's very artistic and loves nature and gardening. Dad could grow an incredible amount of fruits and vegetables, even making his own wine from the grapes and elderberries he grew. Dad appreciated travel and showing my brother and me all about our beautiful planet. He taught social studies for many years and was very interested in geography, politics, history, music, and art. My father is extremely intelligent. He's a great artist who can paint or chalk many Van Gogh and Renoir look-alikes, as well as a few other impressionist painters.

Van Gogh Sunflowers

My Family and me

I feel absolutely blessed to have been raised by parents who had so many wonderful strengths. I'll never forget how they would always dance together at parties, festivals, or weddings. Everyone thought they were the cutest couple. They took us to many gem mining spots throughout Georgia, North Carolina, Arkansas, and Colorado when we were kids. And it was their love of gems, fine stones, travel, and art that led my parents to becoming certified gemologists when I was ten. We tumbled our own rocks and gems that we found along dirty river banks and soon amassed a large collection. My parents eventually opened up a Fine Jewelry and Gifts store in Plantation, Florida while continuing to teach. My grandparents ran the store during the school day, and my brother and I cared for the house and prepared dinner nightly. Both of my parents designed jewelry through art and made gorgeous pieces that people are no doubt still wearing to this day.

I had nice homes, good meals, and cute clothes. My parents always had a job, or two, or three. They valued education and pushed me to pursue my degree and fields of work. We traveled often as a family. We had the privilege of touring our beautiful USA by van - a "Big Orange" van. That's what we called it and it became our CB name, "Breaker Breaker 1-9, Big Orange here looking for Gold Streak". That was my Grandpa and Grandma Allen's van and they traveled with us often during the summers. At nights, my parents slept in the conversion machine while my brother and I slept in tents during our long journeys. There are so many memories!

The Big Orange

Cruise to the Bahamas

Some trips we flew to tropical places like Hawaii, California, or Mexico and others far away like Canada, London, Scotland, and Wales, England. I was so blessed to meet people from different cultures and to experience new lifestyles and ways of doing things. Travel became addicting and I continue to go off on adventures as often as possible today. In addition to our trips, my parents had a timeshare in Kissimmee, Florida for over 10 years, so we have been to Disney World over 50 times. Epcot, Magic Kingdom, Sea World, and Busch Gardens were frequented yearly so the thrill of roller coasters and live shows have always brought me happiness. We spent many weekends in the Florida Keys fishing, boating, sun tanning, or enjoying the nightlife and amazing sunsets. I was very lucky!

2nd grade

During my school years, I got mostly A's and B's, remained on the Honor Roll and in the Honor Society, but I wasn't what we called a "Goody Goody". For Kindergarten, I went to the school where my mom taught 2nd Grade in North Miami. There were only a handful of white kids in this school, but I loved all of my classmates despite the color of their skin. The next year, we moved into a new neighborhood in Sunshine Ranches, close to the everglades in South Florida. Then, I went to three different elementary schools close to our new home because the boundaries kept changing in our home district. We were in the "Boonies", short for the boondocks. My 1st Grade teacher, Mrs. Baker had a major influence on me becoming a teacher. Her dedication and fun-loving personality were unmatched and I wanted to be just like her. Mrs. Hogan, my 5th grade teacher, was amazing as well. I was asked every day to buy her coffee from the cafeteria, given a safety patrol position, and was selected to attend Sea Camp in the Florida Keys with some of my peers. You could say that I was a teacher's pet most of my school years. More about my amazing teacher-experiences will come in my third book that I am dedicating to my teaching and learning life. I've had some wonderful teachers over the years, and I want to celebrate them separately, along with my exciting teaching experiences in Florida and Michigan.

My love life was busy and indecisive. I seemed to jump around from boyfriend to boyfriend during my teens. I met boys at school, work, the beach, or even the mall. My high school surfer boyfriends all taught me patience, as I waited for hours lying in the sun soaking up rays while they surfed all day and night. I paid for that later in life, trust me! At forty-nine, I'm constantly having skin cancer surgeries to have basal cell carcinoma removed, leaving me with scars that I try to cover up with makeup. My fair skin was certainly not meant to spend so much time in the Florida sun.

I had several very cool boyfriends, but Alan was the first boy to steal my heart at sixteen. I met him on the Fort Lauderdale Strip in 1988 in a parking lot behind a pizza place. My friends and I cruised the strip often in our cars and met all kinds of people. Alan and I both had 2 friends with us that night and we hung out in the pizza parking lot for hours. We were both fond of each other and exchanged numbers that night. Alan and I spent the summer together before my senior year before he returned to McGill University in Montreal, Canada. He was very intelligent, fit, funny, and a great dancer! We stayed in touch for over 10 years and tried to rekindle our romance during summers home or when either of us weren't in a relationship. Alan's parents lived in Boca Raton, Florida where he visited often. He truly was my first love.

I graduated from high school in 1989 with a 3.5 GPA. My brother was going to an expensive art and film school away from home, so my parents wanted me to attend a local community college until my brother completed his schooling. I started taking courses at the Broward Community College in the fall, while working full-time at a clothing store called Units. I became actively involved in DECA, a Fashion Marketing club, by holding the office of Secretary. We held fundraisers and events that made me feel incredibly proud. My club raised money and toys for Toys for Tots. My professor, Dr. Goodwin, took a group of us to attend a day conference with Zig Ziglar, a guru in salesmanship. Dr. Richard Goodwin, nominated me for the Who's Who Among American Junior College Students Award. I went to a ceremony and banquet that honored those of us nominated, and my name is in a red Who's Who book. I felt pretty special and it was nice to be recognized.

That December, my best friend, Cindy, and I took a road trip to Gainesville, Florida to visit her boyfriend who attended the University of Florida. Her boyfriend's roommate, Steve, was exactly my type and I fell in love. We all spent the weekend together and I couldn't believe what a gentleman he was and a pre-med student as well. I loved smart guys with a big heart. Luckily, he was heading down to Miami for the next 3 weeks to spend the holidays with his family, and this was only thirty minutes from me, so I was excited to get to know him better. Steve and I went on many dates in Miami over his break and it was then that I decided to do whatever it took to get me accepted into the University of

Florida. I wanted to be near Steve and so I was determined to be a Florida Gator. He was studying to be a doctor, was the valedictorian of his high school, a football player, adorable, and had the most generous and thoughtful heart. For the next few months, I studied for the SAT and took it two more times until I had a decent enough score that would get me into UF. I told Dr. Goodwin that I met a special young man who attended the University of Florida and I wanted to transfer there next fall. He gave me tips and hints that would help get me noticed above the rest. Dr. Goodwin told me to send in a picture of myself, a handwritten essay, and recommendation letters from current professors with my application to the universities I desired to attend. He offered and I accepted, as he wrote me a wonderful recommendation letter that I am still grateful for today.

Cindy and me dressed in Gator Gear

I was accepted into the fall term, 1990, at the University of Florida as a transfer student. Steve and I could finally be together and live in the same town. He spoiled me for two and a half years. Unfortunately, my age and insecurities got the best of me during my third year in college and my mistakes led to our sad break up in 1992. It took a long time for me to forgive myself for losing him - a great catch! Steve loved me and showed me every day. I thought my chances of ever meeting a great guy were over.

Well, I managed to live without Steve for the next couple of years and focused on exercise, friends, and graduating so I could begin my teaching career. I made some great friends during my last couple of years in college and I graduated with a 3.875 GPA, High Honors from the University of Florida and this made me feel very proud, because I had done it all on my own. Early that spring of 1994, I was recruited by the Palm Beach County School Board and offered a job teaching special-education before I had even graduated. I signed the contract and began my teaching career in Boca Raton, Florida a few months later in August of 1994.

Graduated from University of Florida with High Honors 1994

My first five years of teaching students with a variety of exceptionalities were quite challenging, but I loved my job and my students. I made some great friends at work and started living in apartments on my own. I was spending weekends in South Florida at clubs or fancy dinners, taking many road trips with friends and living the single life. I rescued a dog from the Humane Society, and named her Ginger! I felt safer knowing that I had a dog at home when living on my own in my twenties.

In 1999, I had a computer to browse the internet and decided to try online dating, as I felt like I already knew all of the single people who frequented the same bars I went to on the weekends. I wanted to settle down and start a family, so I created a profile and met my son's father, Mick. He's 6'4" with blue eyes and brown hair, a job, condo, and a jet ski.

Soon after, I moved to Southeast Michigan in 2000. I followed Mick when he received a job transfer from Florida to Michigan, so we could begin a new life together right after my parents divorced. We settled down and had a beautiful son, Matthew. I taught special education students in several elementary schools for eighteen years, studied Literacy at Eastern Michigan University and became a Science Liaison Special Education Teacher in a local high school for the past few years. My son is now sixteen and an amazing young man. I was not blessed with any other children, but feel lucky enough to have him by my side.

Michigan remains our home and we have many friends here.

It sounds like I have my shit together over here, doesn't it? These are all facts that make up my timeline. This is what most people know about me - the surface of who I am. Well, there's some deep doo doo that I haven't mentioned and it builds my story and life's purpose.

A Little About Me

WHEN I WAS BORN, it was a miracle. My strong mother didn't give up on me. For some reason, I have had a very exciting life for someone who wasn't even supposed to be born. It was as if my mother left a spark of determination and an everlasting courage in me when the doctors told her to give me up during her fifth month of pregnancy, but she refused. For four months, my mother was on bed rest and insisted on taking the hormone "progesterone", to protect and supplement her body from bleeding too much and risk losing me. My mother lost another child, Michael, who was born a stillbirth prior to my birth. My older brother, John, is two years and two months older than me and was my parents' first child. I was born in the gorgeous and tropical Miami, Florida. My actual birth date is October 31st, 1971 - thirty days after Walt opened Disney World's Magic Kingdom in Kissimmee, Florida. I was a healthy, ten-pound baby girl, named Wendy, born on Halloween. Yes, I have been asked if I'm a good witch or a bad witch - many, many times. My body decided to make its appearance in life, six days after my due date of October 25th. I was clearly in no rush to show my little face to the world. I would soon be tattered, worn, sad, scared, alone, abused, ignored, confused, lied to, neglected, hurt, wrinkled, broke, beat, and definitely pooped on. I took the right path. I could have gone down a much darker road. But I'm still here, smiling and trying to make a difference in the lives of children, my family, and my friends. My hopes are that after reading my book, you too will feel the courage to overcome all the crap that gets stuck on your shoe or gets Pooped in your Pink Patent Leather Purse.

Image © Pinterest

My parents' children, Johnny, Michael, and Wendy were all named after the characters in Peter Pan. My Mom and Dad were both amazing educators in South Florida for over thirty years. My

Mom loved reading Disney stories to her students and her children. She bought us all of the books and records that read the stories to us with voice and enthusiasm. They had beautiful, orchestrated music that accompanied the stories as well, and a cute "ding" to turn the page.

Peter Pan was her favorite of them all and has become mine as well. My mom reminds me of Peter Pan, so I love this story even more. She has led a life of courage, adventure, and authenticity. In addition, I had a friend named Peter who showed up many times during my teen years and twenties in different locations for ten years until his unfortunate death in 1997. You will read about him later and Peter's significance in my life.

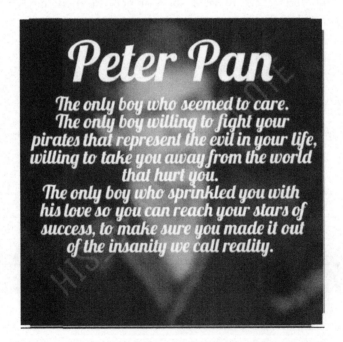

As I reflect on each story from my life that brought me pain or joy, it has turned me into who I am today. I do not feel things lightly anymore. I see right through BS. I am not a fool anymore. I will stand up for myself and advocate for what I want or what I need to be happy, as well as advocate for my loved ones. A close and dear friend, Kathleen, who has known me for twenty years recently told me that I'm a "no-nonsense" kind of gal. I agree with her. With all that I have been through in my last 50 years, I am truly grateful for so many of my guardian angels who have inspired me to continue to wake up every day. I strive, daily, to give the people who I encounter my absolute best self - no matter what life has thrown my way. There are some truly magnificent people out there who have shown me that I am important and that I matter in this world, especially when I didn't believe it. My second book will be filled with praise and honor towards those who have inspired me to live every day. I live with hopes that I will meet more of these people in my next fifty years! There have also been people who have made me feel like a piece of crap on the bottom of a shoe or the smooshed bug stuck to it - even worse, trust me.

I've dedicated my life and time trying to understand why people do what they do and why they act certain ways. Why are some people so insensitive and mean? The ego is a dangerous thing and needs to be tamed.

Me, too. Me, too! I want to yell this from the top of my lungs, but I have been too shy, too reserved, and too fearful of unnecessary judgement and betrayal. No one wants to be judged by their peers or complete strangers for what life throws in their arena. I have kept secrets for so many years about things that happened to me that I did not choose, and I have only chosen a few people to share my stories with; people I trust or people who I think are true friends and won't think differently of me. As soon as the truth comes out, people tend to put labels on those who are courageous enough to tell their stories. I see this too often, especially with women. But how does one get support if they keep it all locked up for so many years fear of being judged?

As soon as I open my mouth, I feel vulnerable. Having the courage to be yourself, and to feel vulnerable when you do, is a crucial part of life and healing. No one has to accept the consequences of my actions - except for me. No one knows how much I can handle or tolerate - except for me. I make my own choices and have selected certain people to be a part of my journey. But there were a lot of things I did not ask for in my life that I have been judged for. The pain this caused me, led me down difficult roads. There have been people who came into my life only to teach me about the darkness, and even though I've pushed them out of my life, they had never really left my thoughts until I found the courage and time to write this book. Here is my truth. Here is my story. This is who I am and why I am the way that I am. All that matters is how I feel in the end, and right now I feel like a champion. I still have the other half of my life to live.

Chapter 1: The Early Crap

BEING BORN on Halloween with the name "Wendy" automatically gave me the nickname, "Wendy the Witch" and allowed my only brother to be disappointed with me since day-one. I'm pretty sure he never forgave me since my parents were at the hospital instead of trick or treating with him on his third Halloween. I was happy to have a brother, though. We spent a lot of time together growing up and I love him very much, even though I always felt like he couldn't stand me and wished me dead.

It was pretty shitty for my mom's doctors to tell her that I wouldn't make it into this world alive, but she didn't give up on me. She didn't want to lose another child and her courage to keep me alive, lives inside me to this day.

Me with my Dad as Santa, 1973

Then, I almost died when I was two years old. My mom gave me a Dum Dum lollipop, and I was so excited I started running. I was prancing around my living room in my long nightgown with ruffles lacing the bottom, and my pink fuzzy slippers. I tripped on the carpet edge and started choking on my lollipop as it slid down my throat. Luckily my Mom heard and saw me close by. She was scared and tried to remove the lolly from my throat, but it didn't budge. She had to pick me up from my feet and turn me upside down while shaking me to dislodge the sucker. My blonde curls were bouncing onto the carpet and my face was turning blue - I couldn't breathe.

My mom was so worried, but she didn't give up! She laid me on the shag carpet and put two of her fingers down my throat and pulled out the butterscotch Dum Dum and it flew across the room. She caught a deep breath and counted her blessings that day - and she never gave me a little sucker again. As I reflect and play detective, and after being educated on the topic, I realize that this event was probably the start of my anxiety and PTSD. The feeling of not being able to breathe can trigger trauma in your brain. At such a young age when the brain is developing, it impacts how we react to our environment. Fight or flight. The lack of oxygen may have had some effects, as well.

My brother, John, and me in 1974

Growing up in the nice South Florida climate kept me outdoors most of the time. I was very outdoorsy, creative, observant, and feminine, but athletic and sporty to survive around my brother and the other boys in the hood. The world was our playground and I loved to play. Like most three-year-old little girls, I enjoyed playing house, dressing up in my mom's clothes, dancing, and playing with dolls, but I also loved fishing and doing "boy stuff" with my brother and his friends. For my third birthday, my Grandma Allen bought me the prettiest pink patent leather purse and I put my new wax lip gloss inside with a pink plastic comb. It had a magnet button to keep it closed and a long strap for me to carry my new favorite gift all over. And I did. I took this purse everywhere I went, and I cherished the pink shiny patent leather material. I especially cherished this purse, because it was my first ever, and it was from my Grandma Allen, who I loved so dearly.

One afternoon after a rainstorm, my brother and I decided to play out back behind our modest Miramar home where there were new houses being built. Johnny, Charlie, and Phillip were playing cops and robbers with wooden rubber band guns while Sarah and I made mud pies with my Betty Crocker mini baking pans. I had my new pink patent leather purse on my shoulder since I was pretending to be a mom, baking. We all know how important it is to have a purse on your arm in case your fake wax lip gloss gets licked off or fades in the sun. I was prepared, just in case. Sarah and I made mud pies with shells as decorations for the top, designed into a creative pattern. For some reason, we didn't mind getting our hands dirty, since the hose was easy to turn on and hooked to the back of my house. We were proud of our hard work, so my friend and I wanted our fancy pies to bake in the hot Florida sun for the evening. Johnny and I got called in for bathing and dinner soon afterwards. We both raced to the hose to rinse off the mud from the rain earlier in the day. He knocked me over and I fell to the ground with my pink patent leather purse that I held

Phillip Pooped in my Pink Patent Leather Purse

onto tightly. I hung it up on the hose faucet and rinsed my crunchy hands until most of the brown dirt washed off into the grass. Next, I rubbed my feet and ankles while rinsing them under the faucet as well, until I could only see the grass stains on my knees. I stood in a small lake of brown water that the spigot left behind. Again, my mother called Johnny and me to dinner, so we rushed inside to see what deliciousness she had whipped up in the kitchen. She was always a great cook!

I don't remember what exactly we had for dinner that night. Once I was in the shower getting washed up with soap and rinsing off the potential ringworm, I realized that I left my new favorite purse outside by the faucet. After dinner I begged my mom to let me go outside and get my pink shiny bag, but she declined since it was getting dark. "Don't worry, I saw Phillip out behind our house cleaning up in our hose before he left, and he wouldn't touch it." My mother loved purses, and still does, so I'm surprised she didn't let me go outside to retrieve my precious item. But my mom was the type of parent who kept her word. If she said NO, then even if she realized she was being too harsh, she'd keep her word and stick to NO. "No means No, not 'maybe'", was a common phrase we heard often. My brother and I were relentless at times though. But all I could think about was my new pink precious purse that I wanted to put on my dresser that night so I could admire it from my bed. Not to mention my new waxy lip gloss that made me feel so grown up, and the comb I use for my dolls' hair as I tuck them into bed. Oh well, I decided that I'll run out first thing in the morning since I was afraid of the dark anyways.

The next day was sunny and bright with a bit of dew on the long grass near our home. We were packing up to head to Dania Beach for the day when I remembered that I had to retrieve my pink patent leather purse. I ran out through the glass sliding doors onto the hot chattahoochee patio, through the screen door, and out onto the grass near the faucet. I saw my prized possession hanging in the same spot where I had left it and I was so happy to know that no one had taken my treasure overnight. I grabbed the shiny strap and pulled the pink preciousness off the faucet hook, noticing that it was a bit heavier than before. I thought maybe it got water inside from the faucet and noticed a little brown mark from our mud pie adventure the day prior. I got concerned about my lip gloss so I checked to see if it was still okay and usable. As I peeked into the shiny pink pocketbook, took a regretful sniff, I could not believe what I saw. I dropped it into the wet brown grass immediately and cried. Someone pooped in my pink patent leather purse! Phillip Pooped in my Pink Patent Leather Purse! Even though I was only three at the time, I was pissed!! Haven't trusted boys ever since. Real poop in my favorite purse. Disgusting. Not okay. It must have been convenient for Phillip to use something so precious to me as a toilet.

Thank you, Phillip. Thank you for starting this curse of being pooped on literally and figuratively

for the rest of my life. I know it was you, Phillip.

Five years old and potty trained but locked out of his house, Phillip was that dirty kid in the neighborhood who didn't get called home for dinner. His faucet bath was the only bath he got that day. Kids learn how to treat people by how they are treated by those they love.

We moved about six months later.

Image © Pinterest

Chapter 2:
If I Was a Bird

AT FOUR, I attended pre-school while my mother taught elementary school in Miami. I believe it was called, Small Fry. I remember having a male teacher who wore a pink shirt, and I thought that was silly. My dad never wore pink and I thought it was just for girls. My mother dressed me in beautiful dresses with adorable lines of ruffles on the back of my panties. I had the white woven knee high socks with pom-poms and black patent leather Mary Janes. This was what I wore every day to Small

Fry until the day I sat crying embarrassingly while I waited for my Mom to pick me up.

The monkey bars were part of our recess playground and I loved to swing from ring to ring pretending there was an alligator in the woodchip-water below. My imagination would encourage me to grab and hold on tight so I didn't fall into the gator's mouth, just like in Peter Pan. There was a boy who was in my class, whose name I cannot remember, who chased me around the playground wanting to play house with me. As I was running away from him one day, I jumped onto the monkey bars and swung across like an orangutan going after a banana. My pom-poms from my socks were swinging with me as I reached for each bar. That intrusive young boy ran under the monkey bars and looked right up my dress. He pointed at my ruffled panties and laughed. Everyone around him looked. I dropped down and ran to the bench where I hid my face in tears until my mom picked me up. I didn't like being laughed at. I was humiliated. On another day at preschool, one of the kids ripped the little pom pom balls off my socks, leaving a big hole at the top, near my knee. I hated having this hole in my sock. I thought everyone could see it and would laugh at me. This caused me to feel shame and anxiety for some reason.

At this age, I started having bad night terrors and thinking that my dolls were going to come alive at night and kill me. Maybe it was because I watched scary shows like Paradise Island. I had to jump two feet to get onto my bed because the monsters, people, dolls, whatever it was underneath my bed, might grab my legs and pull me under. I was afraid of the dark and hated the nights. I would beg my brother to sleep in my room with me or let me sleep in his bed with him most nights. I always slept with a night light on, music, or book on tape. These are signs of childhood anxiety.

I've always loved clothes, shoes, purses, makeup, and fashion in general. I spent a lot of time thinking about what to wear every day and my style has always reflected my personality. At the age of four, I thought I could be a Broadway dancer, fashion designer, or fashion model. I loved paper dolls and Barbies. I had the best collection and drew my own dresses with unique patterns.

At five, we moved to Davie, Florida, Sunshine Ranches, rodeo town, just a few minutes east of the Everglades National Park. My mom had me attend the elementary school where she was teaching in North Miami for kindergarten. I remember being the only white girl in my class. The black kids would touch my hair and face as if they had never seen a white person before.

Maybe they hadn't. As we drove through the neighborhood to get to school, we saw iron gates to keep others out of their yards, windows, and doors on the houses and it made me feel worried. Regardless, I loved my classmates, all of them, despite the color of their skin, because they always treated me with kindness. My mom was a 2nd Grade teacher at this school and my teacher was my mom's best friend, Mrs. Kornfield. Even her name reminded me of a peaceful cornfield and I questioned the spelling, even back then. I remember losing my little white sweater one day at school and of course I was crying about it. Mrs. Kornfield was so kind to me, as she took me in her arms and lovingly helped me look everywhere for it until we found it. To this day, forty-five years later, I still connect with Mrs. Kornfield and cherish her like family. She remembers me as the little girl with the lost white sweater. She has always inspired me to be kind to others when they look lost or to help those in need without hesitating. She is one of the reasons I became a teacher.

Home in neighborhood near my mom's work

Moving ahead, about two years later, I attended 2nd Grade at a local school with the other children in my neighborhood of Sunshine Ranches. We lived in Broward County and my parents worked in Dade County, so there were a few days a year that our home district didn't have school, but my parents did. On those days, my brother and I would go to work with one of my parents and get to know their students and fellow staff members. I usually played teacher by practicing writing my letters with chalk on paint lined blackboards or giving my brother math problems to figure out. One day when it was a teacher's work day for my mom, no students were in the building, I snuck outside onto the PE field and jumped on the monkey bars. Afraid that someone might be watching me, I moved over to the uneven bars to flip around on one leg. When I swung my legs and body upwards, my eyes locked onto the car and the man waiting by the gate a few hundred feet away. He started yelling, "Hey little girl, hey little girl, come for a ride with me. No one will know." He started walking closer to me, so I jumped down and ran as fast as I could to find a door to the school that opened. I didn't say a word to him or turn back - ever.

Phillip Pooped in my Pink Patent Leather Purse

All the doors were locked on the outside of the building to get back into the school near the field. My heart was racing and beating so fast, I was so scared. I finally jumped the fence near the front of the school building and made it to the entrance that was unlocked. I was safe. I never told anyone because I wasn't supposed to be outside. I asked my brother if I could sleep in his room that night because I was scared. He let me sleep at the foot of his bed, all curled up safe and sound, smelling his stinky feet. I did this for years to come.

"Hey little girl, come for a ride with me."

Chapter 3: Poop Happens

I DIDN'T ALWAYS get along with my brother. Even though I loved and still love him dearly, we had our moments. He'd call me hurtful names and chase me with frogs - I despise frogs from growing up near the everglades where there were frogs-a-plenty. My brother liked to show me who the boss was and order me around telling me to make him food and clean up after him.

He'd chase me with knives around the house and tell me that he'd kill me if I told mom or dad the "bad" things he did. You know, typical sibling rivalry. No matter how bad or mean he was to me, I still wanted to hang with him at night in his room, even if he didn't want me there. My brother could be very sweet sometimes. He's an artist and is so talented and imaginative. We had some very happy memories making up plays and musicals for the neighbors. He could draw or paint anything! He painted a big unicorn on my wall to match my bedspread, sleeping bag, bathing suit, and pretty much everything else I owned at that time. I believed in magic then, true love, and unicorns.

My brother and I had many friends in our neighborhood in Southwest Ranches. It was horse, pony, ATC trailing, pool, and trampoline fun most of the time with the other kids who lived on an acre and a half near us. Some of my best friends in this neighborhood were Rene, Kim, Jack, Todd, Tina, and Shelley to name a few. We lived near canals, treed lots, and bike and horse trails near the everglades. We spent a lot of time outside, barefoot, wild, free, and surrounded by nature. Despite the frogs, snakes, cockroaches, and heavy mosquitoes, it was the best place to grow up. Everything was great living in the ranches until we lost our best friend, Todd.

When I was six, Todd and his brother, Brad, moved in three houses down from us. I spent a lot of time over at Todd's because his mom, Jackie, was so nice to me. I remember that they always had the most beautiful Christmas tree. It was a white tree with tinsel and it seemed magical to me when I was a young girl. I'd always go home and get excited when I found a little piece of tinsel attached to my clothes. My parents didn't use tinsel, because it was too messy. When Todd's mom became pregnant with his little sister, Paige, I became her little sidekick and wanted to help with Paige when she was a baby. Todd and I grew to be very good friends and even more one day. One summer, when I was about nine or ten, Todd and I were playing house and he and I were the husband and wife, while Paige was our new baby. After playing inside for a while and Paige was taking her nap, Todd decided to get a sheet and tie the corners around trunks of big trees on the side of his yard. We wanted to create a sheet fort in the trees, but it turned out more like a hammock that forced us to be very close together. We laid in the homemade hammock, and I could feel his breath on me while lying there with him. I kind of liked it. Todd and I talked about how moms and dads kiss each other and we decided that we should try it. I mean, we were playing house and we had to act like real parents. Todd was a good looking boy, only a few months older than me. He always had bushy but shiny brown hair, a tan face from being outside so much, and a slightly pudgy build from his mom's good cookin'. He was so funny and fun to be with. I cared for Todd very much, enough to make him my husband while playing house. Even enough to allow him to be my first kiss. Right there in the light blue homemade sheet hammock, we kissed over and over until we had a thirty-second kiss of flat lips, no tongue kissing. We even counted in our heads for thirty seconds. I remember us starting with a quick peck on the lips, then Todd wanted to keep holding it longer. So we thought it would be fun to kiss a little bit longer each time, increasing by five second increments. I decided it was okay because I saw it on soap operas and I was intrigued. I trusted Todd. We both agreed to each kiss and how long each one would be. We worked our way up to a thirty-second kiss. It was harder than you think. Holding our breath or not giggling were our challenges. There were many quiet moments while resting in that light blue sheet hammock with my pretend husband, Todd, that day. I watched the rays of sun peek through the skinny pine branches, listened to the birds flying overhead or at rest in the trees with us. Not a care in the world. It was so peaceful and freeing. I kissed a boy. I didn't have to use my tongue like they did on TV. Todd was like my best friend with long kiss benefits. We could talk about life or remain silent together and it was always perfect. He had a very kind soul that didn't get angry. We practiced being quiet together when we'd go fishing in the canals close by. Todd and I got better at building sheet forts and hammocks that summer and we didn't share our secrets of playing house and kissing like husband and wife, minus the tongue. When we were eleven, the Rocky III movie came out and he loved the song, "Eye of the Tiger". We would dance and sing to it, when it came on the radio. I still think of Todd every time I hear that song. It reminds me to be a champion and to not give up. I would like this song played at my funeral.

As time went by, Todd and I remained close friends, but he fell in love with another girl a couple of years later who lived a few blocks away. Her name is Crystal and she had very white blonde hair, like crystals. I wasn't heart-broken, because I had a crush on a cool rocker boy who wore metal tees and skipped school. I was in middle school and was intrigued by the burnouts, though I didn't smoke pot myself. I still hung out with Todd and his siblings when I went to help his mom with Paige. She was like my little sister, and I loved her dearly. I would always think of Todd when I walked through our secret spot in the trees next to his house where we kissed. I would turn red just thinking about our long kisses and his respect for me.

One sunny day in August, 1983, after a long rain the day prior, my brother and I invited Todd to come with us to our parents' jewelry store in Plantation, FL, so we could go fishing in the New River Canal. It was a popular spot for fishing and my brother and I knew how much Todd loved to fish. My parents became gemologists that year and opened up a Fine Jewelry and Gifts shop in a strip mall. They had this store for several years paired with teaching full time in another county. My grandparents ran the jewelry store during the day and my parents took over on the evenings and weekends. Johnny and I were expected to spend time at the store with my parents so we didn't kill each other if they left us home alone. We of course wanted to be with our friends in the ranches, so sometimes we were allowed to invite a friend to hang out with us during the day. That day, Todd's mom said, "No". Todd had to stay home and do yard work instead, so he was unable to come fishing with us. We were bummed, but we went to my parents' shop anyway. Johnny had just turned fifteen and I was going to be thirteen that October. I had no idea that it would be one of the worst years of my life and that I was going to feel grief and sorrow for the first time.

My brother, Johnny and I were hanging out at the Wicker and Rattan furniture store with the salespeople when we got called back to my parents' store. We made friends with so many of the store employees in the plaza. It would give us something to do when we had to be there on the weekends or long summer days and it kept us out of trouble, I think. My dad came to the Wicker and Rattan store and said you need to come back to our shop right now so we can tell you some news. It was about two o'clock in the afternoon and the sun was shining, but there was a dark cloud waiting to pass. I didn't know what my dad was about to tell me. I was worried about my grandparents, because I was so close to them. When Johnny and I got back to the store, my parents told us to sit down. I covered my mouth slightly with my hand and waited to hear the news. "Todd went to heaven today. He was trying to climb his rope on the swing set and it wrapped around his neck. The stool he was standing on sunk into the ground and Todd couldn't pull himself up. The other rope wrapped around his neck. He accidentally hung himself in his backyard. His mom found him when she looked out her back window and he was already dead." I just sat there in shock with my hand over my mouth, thinking this can't be happening. This can't be real. I must be dreaming.

I cried a lot that month. Most of the time I cried by myself in my room. Todd's funeral was so sad. All of his family was there and all of the kids from the neighborhood who loved him so much. He had no enemies. Todd was everyone's best friend and we were all heartbroken by his passing. Todd was buried in his brand new Jordache Jeans and Ocean Pacific t-shirt that he was planning on wearing the first day of 7th Grade. I will never forget that day and how much it rained the night of his funeral. I knew that the angels were crying for us, but glad to receive such a kind soul in heaven.

But we were expected to just move on and live our lives trying to understand why bad things happen to good people. I felt so sad for myself for losing such a great friend, but I couldn't help but think of how Todd's Mom, Jackie, felt about losing her precious son and finding him dead out her kitchen window. That scene never leaves my mind. I learned empathy through this experience. I spent a lot of time with Jackie and Paige after Todd's death. Jackie would just hold me and cry on my shoulder. Sometimes we'd cry together. I felt like she was so alone in her struggle because she was expected to care for everyone else, but she could no longer take care of herself. Todd just had this presence about him that we all missed. He lit up a room and now we all have to live without that light. It was so hard. For about a year and a half, I tried to spend time over there bringing some light to Todd's family. I'm not sure I ever really grieved enough over this loss.

My sweet friend, Todd Gilpin

Chapter 4:
Unlucky 13 Crap

A FEW MONTHS later, life seemed to go back to "normal" in the ranches. My friend, Rene, asked me to go ATC riding through some trails to visit some friends in another neighborhood. We had just gotten out of my pool, so we were in our bathing suits and used our towels like sarongs so we could walk to her house respectfully. Since my parents didn't allow us to have motorized vehicles for toys, I was of course cautious about riding her ATC by myself. I didn't tell my parents I was going riding, because they would say NO! Rene used her brothers ATC and I rode her red 3-wheeler through the trails following her. It was so much fun driving through the dirt trails, dodging tree limbs and sharp bushes, and going up and down big hills. Once we got to another hood nearby, Sunshine Ranches, we drove around to visit our friends. And after swimming at Michelle's, we decided to go home in our bathing suits to let them air dry in the sun. I was thirteen, but looked sixteen. I had long legs and was taller than most 13-year-old girls. I was also naive, innocent, prude, and afraid of boys. While we were driving home through Sunshine Ranches, we noticed a royal blue Camaro driving around with teenage boys inside.

Kim, Rene, and me at 13

Phillip Pooped in my Pink Patent Leather Purse

They would drive near us and whistle, yell things at us to get our attention, and make comments about our bathing suits. I hated it. It made me so nervous. I was a virgin, driving around as an inexperienced ATC driver, nervous as heck. The last thing I needed was a group of boys in a car making comments about me in my bathing suit. As we drove our ATCs to get away from the boys, they kept chasing us in their car thinking it was funny. I followed Rene down a long paved road going full throttle until we got to the dirt road that led us to the trail to our neighborhood. I felt immense pressure to get away from these boys as I knew they were older and I did not know their intentions. My heart beat fast and I was afraid of the unknown. As I turned onto the dirt road, I didn't slow down or shift down enough, so I flipped the ATC several times after sliding sideways in the dirt and into a ditch covered with barbed wire. I couldn't get up without help. My body was cut from head to toe from the barbed wire. The boys in the car saw my accident and stopped to see if they could help. I was sure to tell them that it was because of them that I flipped and got hurt. I yelled at them to stay away. Rene stopped her ATC and came running so fast to see if I was okay. My ankle was swollen to the size of a softball and I couldn't walk on it. I had cuts all over my body. I was afraid to go home. My parents were going to a Tom Jones concert that night and I knew how much they were looking forward to it. The ATC I was riding stopped running and the tire was all jacked up, so Rene had to tie a rope from her ATC to mine and towed me back to her house while I sat on the ATC. My ankle hurt every time we hit a bump. It seemed like the longest ride back to Rene's house. When we got there, I took a shower and borrowed some of Rene's clothes to cover up my scrapes, cuts, and purple swollen ankle. I did not want my parents to know that anything bad happened to me because they would have to go to the hospital instead of the Tom Jones concert. Rene took me home later, where I went right to my room and stayed there until my parents left for the night. After they had left, my ankle grew darker and darker, bigger and bigger. I hobbled next door to a neighbor's house who gave me ice packs to keep on it all night. When my parents came home around two o'clock in the morning, I woke up and showed them my ankle, cuts, etc. … and they took me to the emergency room right away. The ER doctor said I tore ligaments in my ankle and would have to walk on crutches with an ace bandage for a few weeks. It was so purple and painful. I had to use crutches at school and got to leave class early to get from class to class with a friend carrying my books. My cuts of course eventually healed, but they left scars that I still see today. I was so mad at those boys. I wished they would have just left us alone.

My follow-up doctor's appointment was on my thirteenth birthday, so I got out of school a little early to go find out updates on my ankle with an X-ray. I was told that I would need a white plaster cast and would have to continue using my crutches for eight more weeks. It was my thirteenth birthday. It was Halloween. It was raining that night. Plaster casts and crutches don't do so well in the rain. I was unable to go trick or treating with my friends on my birthday. So everyone left me at home that night to have some neighborhood fun, except for my grandparents. I remember my Grandpa Allen noticing how sad I was, so he put on fake plastic glasses with the nose on the end and followed me around that night trying to make me laugh. It worked. I never forgot his kindness. My 15-year-old brother came home late that night, past his curfew, smelling of alcohol and cigarettes. My dad was absolutely pissed. Curse words were exchanged and that was not common in our home. The next thing I knew, my brother and dad were in a fist fight on the floor in the living room… again, on my thirteenth birthday. It sucked, to say the least. My brother ended up running away from home that night, so I didn't sleep a wink. A few days later he tapped on my window asking for food. He told me he was living in the trees behind our house. Eventually, after a few more days, he came back home until the eventual next time he got caught doing something that upset my parents. I told you it was one of the worst years of my life. It does get better though.

A few months later, once my ankle was healed and I was able to prance around with my neighborhood friends again, my bad luck with guys named Mick began while I was still thirteen years old. A group of us were actually hanging out at Todd's house with his brother, Brad, and some other kids who lived close by. Truth or Dare was a popular game that teens played for kicks and giggles. I was in 8th Grade and had never French-kissed a guy, so one of our neighbors named Mick, who thought he was hot stuff, dared me to French-kiss him. I was of course known as the prude one in the neighborhood so I think he did it just to see if he could. I don't remember the kiss that much other than it was fast and weird. Mick came out of the dare telling everyone that I bit his lip. I did no such thing. I would have known if I had bitten his lip. I couldn't help but question his need for telling everyone a lie. I know I didn't bite his lip during my first French-kiss and I was devastated when he told everyone I had. Of course, you know how schools spread rumors. Well, it went all over the school and I was humiliated. I hated this Mick guy for trying to be so cool and lie to everyone just to make me look bad. Joke's on me. Ha ha. I was still not over the loss of Todd, still didn't trust boys since the accident, and now the rumors. I hated living in that neighborhood. I just wanted to hide from everyone and not show my face.

The next spring, when my Mom was cleaning our house, she bent over to pick up a fallen toothbrush holder, and she couldn't get up. After a trip to the emergency room, we found out that she had slipped three discs in her back and needed surgery. It was a major surgery and she was in the hospital for a couple of weeks. She had to recuperate for a few months more on bed rest during the summer while we tried to sell our home in the ranches. My mom is a very hard worker and after her surgery, we all knew it was time to leave our home on the one and a half acres. We were going to miss this home with woods and so many kinds of fruit trees that my dad had planted. All around the perimeter of our backyard, my dad built a fence and grew grape vines along it. He planted avocado, lime, kumquat, banana, oranges, and elderberry trees. He made wine out of the elderberries, grapes, and kumquats, and we often ate the fruits of his labor. We also had a very nice pool that kept us cool all summer in our private large yard.

I have near-endless memories of this home and many are wonderful, but they are being overtaken by the heartbreaking ones. I would miss the many friends who I adored, but I was ready to leave. I was ready to begin a new chapter. I was ready to not be the Wendy that was so sad from losing her best friend and the girl who bit a boy's lip during a French-kiss. Goodbye big, beautiful home in Sunshine Ranches. You brought us so many memories for nine years.

Phillip Pooped in my Pink Patent Leather Purse

Chapter 5:
It's About to Go Down

I LOST MY virginity at the age of fourteen, but not by choice, a couple of months after moving into our new neighborhood in Davie, FL. We had to move into a home with lawn maintenance included so my parents chose to move into a small townhome about twenty minutes from our old neighborhood. It was close to busy roads and other apartments and condos. It was nothing like the ranches, but there was a pool, racquetball, and tennis courts for community residents to keep busy.

I was not ready to have sex and I didn't even like the man who I gave up my virginity to. It was a time when I lacked courage and did not scream the way I wanted to. I did not have a voice yet.

I was tall, 5'9" with long blonde hair, blue eyes, and freckled tan skin. I loved to dance, run, and eat good food, so I kept in shape. My brother and I became instantly popular as the new kids on our block. It was easy to make new friends there because this was the 80's and we spent time outside with our friends. One guy had his eye on me and it was known all over the new hood that Mick, a 19-year-old, wanted to be my boyfriend. I rode the bus to school in 9th Grade and his sister went to my high school. Every day for a few weeks, she would hand me a flower, note, or some kind of gift from Mick. It was very sweet and romantic, but I was a 14-year-old virgin.

This was my first semester in high school. Mick was nineteen years old, very strong and muscular, but not very tall. He wore his hair like a cop, short all the way around. His skin was tanned perfectly from the sun while he worked daily as a landscaper. I did not hold strong feelings for Mick, but he seemed to be crazy about me. He would greet me at my bus stop after school and wanted to spend every minute of his night with me. I remember he would take me for walks to private areas in his apartment complex, sometimes the pool, sometimes by a pond, or on a picnic bench under a pavilion. All he wanted to do was kiss me and try to touch me, but I was a prude and did not want to move fast. It all made me feel uncomfortable. He was putting pressure on me to do things I was not ready for. Mick was not the guy I wanted to lose my virginity to. One night, he took me behind the racquetball court and he disconnected the lights so it would be dark. He made us a private spot between five or six tall pine trees. I was given a spot to sit that was covered in old pine needles. He tried to make out with me and move his fingers between my legs. All I could do was giggle and push his hands away. I didn't have that feeling about Mick that made me want him to touch me or have the privilege of being my first.

All of the people in my neighborhood and my close friends kept telling me how crazy I was for not liking Mick. He was hot and he had a body that the girls in the neighborhood loved. He was romantic and bought me cute and sweet gifts, but something didn't feel right to me. He was nineteen and I was a freshman in high school. I'm still a little girl and he's a man now. I can't do this.

But Mick did not take "no" for an answer. He was persistent. I told him that I wanted to break up with him and he cried like a baby. I told him that I'd give him another chance, but that I needed some space. He showed up at my door two days later with yet another gift for me. He had spent his hard earned paycheck on a 14k gold herringbone chain and a pendant with a heart between both of our initials. It was as if he was branding me. Now I was his and no one else could have me.

My friends and family thought it was a sweet gesture. I wasn't as touched. I knew what he was up to. He was trying to butter me up so I'd have sex with him. He wanted to be my first and I let him one day even though I lay there screaming inside.

One evening, around dusk, the sky was a spooky grey. A storm was coming. Mick took my hand and led me to his apartment. When we walked inside I smelled cigarettes and marijuana. Five people were sitting around a kitchen table under a dim light all looking at something on the table. I can't remember what it was because Mick led me to his room as soon as we entered. He told me that he'd be right back and he closed the door. I looked around the room. He had a couch for a bed, clothes on the floor, and a large cabinet with a stereo and big speakers inside. On the walls were pinned up posters of women in barely-there bikinis. They were women and I was a flat-chested 14-year-old girl who was scared and trapped. What could he want with me?

Within a few minutes, Mick came back into the room locking it behind him. He brought a brown towel that he laid on the floor and a glass of water that he put in the wood cabinet. He told me to lay down on the towel. I did not agree to anything. Mick kneeled near me and wiggled his way to the stereo. He put on Air Supply's greatest hits and was planning his move. I did not want to be there. I told him that I should go home because of the storm. He told me over and over again that everything would be okay and that I didn't have to be afraid. He took off his shirt and was in nothing but a towel wrapped around his waist. He lied on the towel next to me and told me to take off my clothes. I was shaking. I wanted to stay in a t-shirt in case someone came in but he reassured me that the door was locked. I was naked, naive, and cold. Mick wrapped his big strong arms around me and pulled me close. He told me that he was going to pop my cherry so he'd need a towel. I told him I didn't want to have sex. He said I was being a chicken and had nothing to be afraid of. He flipped me onto my back, spread my legs, and jumped on top of me. I wasn't strong enough and I was scared. Mick's towel was off now and his hard body pushed into mine and I cringed because I wanted to scream. I wanted to scream "get off of me, go away, I don't care if I ever see you again". It hurt, because I was so tight and I didn't know what to expect. I was upset that I was allowing that to happen. I'll never forget the music playing. I'll never forget how I felt like I was being raped. I wanted to push him off of me and run, but I was afraid of being laughed at. His hands pushed against mine on the floor and I felt forced to stay there. As I made a slight noise, "ouch", he shushed me and I was told to keep quiet. "It's supposed to hurt", he whispered. I did not love that man. I did not respect that man. He did not respect me. There were no clues from me other than the fact that I didn't run the hell out of there, that told him that I wanted to have sex, that I was enjoying myself, or that I wanted to stay. A tear fell from my eye. I was quiet. I saw the blood on the towel that he purposely put there. I wanted to go home. I told him that I wanted to go home to take a shower and I left. I ran home and didn't look back. I never wanted to see that man again. I was angry. Angry at him, but more angry at myself for allowing it to happen. I was ashamed of myself. I kept this a secret for five years.

I just wanted to be held, loved, and looked at like I was someone special. That's all I really wanted. The only one to have shown me that respect up until then was Todd. But he was gone and we were younger then.

The next day, Mick showed up at our front door. My mom came to my room and told me that Mick was there to see me. I told her that I didn't want to see him and that I wanted to be alone. My brother yelled from his room across the hall, "She's being a little bitch!", and my mom closed the door and left me alone.

The next day, he showed up again and I told my family the same thing. 19-year-old tough guy, Mick, was crying at my door. I was now the bad guy. I was now the "bitch" who was rude to boys who only did nice things for me, according to them. I felt it. I felt the contempt and disgust from my family for making Mick cry. If only everyone knew that I cried about what he did to me for over thirty years. I was not being a bitch. I was standing up for myself. No one knew that.

As a freshman in high school, I had my eye on a boy at school, who's name I do not remember. I wanted to meet a shy guy who would make me feel safe. I went to a high school party after one of the football games a couple of weeks after Mick had his way with me. That cute guy who went to my school was at the party. He stood tall and thin with a lot of brown curls on his head. He dressed very preppy with a navy and white striped polo shirt and jeans, and he was shy but confident. He was not boisterous and seemed to be cool and kind. My friend, Lori, was friends with his friend, Tom, so I decided to stand over by them and see if he showed any interest. Lori was one of my beautiful popular friends who exuded confidence. So of course, all of the cute popular guys liked her. She introduced me to the one I was interested in and we actually started talking. I found out that he races motorbikes and I was intrigued. We started talking and I thought for a moment that I might have a chance with this guy. He was a year older than me so it would look good to have a boyfriend in school that was an upperclassmen. Within a few minutes, I heard a familiar voice from behind me. We were standing under the lights on a tennis court and I was facing the cute guy. The party was at a big house in the ranches and all of the kids were between the deck where the keg was, and on the tennis courts. The familiar voice yelled, "Hey!", and I turned to the right to see who it was right as Mick threw a punch right at the cute guy's jaw and knocked him down to the ground. I was in shock. I turned and ran away.

There was a crowd around the cute guy on the ground and Mick was being pulled away by four big guys. He was trying to fight them off but they made him leave. I grabbed Lori and asked her to drive me home. I started crying and felt helpless. I did not feel safe. I felt humiliated because everyone in my high school now knows that Mick punched the cute guy because he was talking to me. Mick was trying to be possessive of something that didn't belong to him. I couldn't explain to anyone that I wanted to get away from Mick because of his pressure on me to have sex with him and his lack of respect for my personal choice. This was way too complicated and people would probably just think I was a slut if they found out that I had sex. It was not my choice. I wished it had never happened. I've never forgotten the entire scene and have regretted not kicking the guy in the balls and running for my life.

I learned early on that it was safer to just keep to myself since no one will understand me anyway. Nobody asked me why I wanted to be left alone. This is when I started writing letters to God.

Phillip Pooped in my Pink Patent Leather Purse

Every Sunday when I was in 9th Grade, I would lock myself in my room and read the Bible or at least try to understand parts of it. My family did not raise me going to church and I needed some hope. My view of the world at this point in my life was not pretty. I did not see any value in remaining here on earth. Whenever I cried, no one seemed to care. I felt hopeless. It had been very painful so far and I just wanted a better life. I wanted different experiences. I wanted someone to care about me, but instead, I would write letters to God. I would thank him for what I loved and then I would write down my pains and tell God that I am ready to go back. I do not like living in this cruel world. I was not a coward, just hopeful that someone would hear my cry. My family heard me crying sometimes and I would hear, "Oh, the crybaby is in her room crying again." I felt ashamed for being sensitive. I still cry easily and wish it were different.

I had vivid dreams that year that I will never forget. I spent a lot of time in my room by myself, listening to music, writing, and praying for a better life. One night I had a dream that gave me some hope, but it was surreal. I dreamed that I was sliding down a very long dark tunnel that seemed to go on endlessly. But as I finally came to its end, I slowed and stood up before leaving. I saw a very bright light and a body-shaped being of mostly bright light without a clear face at the end of the tunnel. I saw a shining palace behind the body of light, all white and gold and beautiful. The kind and gentle being of light told me that it wasn't my time and I had to stay. I woke up a little enlightened and tried to change my attitude. I guess if it wasn't my time, then I could stop writing the letters to God and deal with life's challenges. It was not easy, but some people made it easier to cope.

Image © SoundCloud

Chapter 6: Hot Shit!

THAT NEXT FALL, I met my high school and lifetime best friend, Cindy, in 10th Grade. We met in a ceramics and pottery class. She was new to our school, and I thought my new friend was funny and always seemed happy. We became inseparable and she became my light during my high school years. Cindy was outgoing, hilarious, strong, and very tall. Together we were pretty awesome. It made us more attractive and she helped me come out of my shell again. Cindy was so fun to be around and absolutely full of life. We always had the best adventures. We are still very close today, thirty-four years later.

As I became confident in myself, the boys became interested. I had boyfriend after boyfriend during my high school years. Usually, I would go out with a guy and then someone better would come along and I dumped them for the next one. I guess I was a heart-breaker. But, I also got my heart broken plenty by my own mind. If I had a crush on someone I thought was too good looking for me or too smart for me, then I didn't do or say anything out of fear of rejection. I was insecure, like many girls. I was protecting my fragile, wrinkled heart. My dating choice was mostly surfers and a few athletes, but I had very high expectations at this point and was easily disappointed. I think I already had PTSD, because I lived in fear constantly and had to work at loving and trusting others. It truly became a job for me to learn how to love. I was not raised in an affectionate home, so the words, "I love you" were rarely exchanged.

I did not think I was smart in high school, though I got good grades and school came easily. I was prettier when laughing, so I became attractive during my high school years, especially when I was with my friends - especially when I was with Cindy. I didn't think I was "all that", because I was taller and curvier than most girls my age. I didn't have the petite cheerleader body and I had to learn to love what I was.

My brother was a surfer and we went to the beach a lot with his friends. I was the beach bunny who got stuck watching everyone's keys, sex wax, and towels while lying out in the sun for several hours while the guys surfed. If I wasn't at the beach during the day, then I was at a pool taking in the rays. Having a nice tan was important in Florida. I of course paid for it all later and wish I had put on more sunscreen.

Phillip Pooped in my Pink Patent Leather Purse

Junior Year 1988

My friends and I enjoyed going to parties and sneaking into clubs passing for twenty-one. I was only sixteen. I loved dancing because it allowed me some release, freedom, and movement. I could feel the music through the floor and it just moved me freely. Being physically fit has always been important to me. Exercising was a part of my daily routine and still remains to be. I have a major sweet tooth and have to exercise or I would gain too much weight to feel good about myself.

One springtime sunny afternoon during my junior year, like many days, I was sitting in a lounge chair in a bikini by the pool, "lying in the sun", we called it. I read in my Self magazine that some women wrapped cling wrap to their legs and this produced more sweat during exercise.

So I tried that one day. Giggle. You're laughing with me...

I went home after the suntan session, and I took my mom's package of cellophane and wrapped several layers around my thighs and arms. I put on some light grey jogging pants with a navy blue tank top and went for a run. It was bikini season, and I wanted to look good and lose the Oreo cookies and Doritos that I loved and ate so often. It was about seven o'clock in the evening. In South Florida, you have to wait until evening to exercise outside, because the humidity and heat are brutal during the day. I jogged about four miles that evening and I could feel the sweat trapped in the cling wrap waiting to be released.

As I was jogging towards home along a busy road, Orange Drive, in Davie, Florida, I was frightened by a station wagon that pulled up next to me. A man, about mid 30s, was driving the white tank with brown wood paneling between the paint job. He pulled up next to me and kept the car at my jogging-pace. There was a young boy, about the age of six, in the backseat looking down and afraid. The man told me to hop in and go for a ride with him and the boy. I kept running, now a little faster thinking that if I ignored him, he'd go away. But the guy kept driving at my pace. I was running out of breath and my street to turn on was coming up, so I slowed down and stopped and let him go ahead of me. That crazy man stopped the station wagon and I ran behind it, turning right and heading into a neighborhood where I could lose him easily. I remember thinking about the little boy in that car! All I could think about at that moment was saving myself. I didn't get a peek at his license plate. I felt so guilty that I couldn't help that little boy. I just turned and ran until I couldn't see a trace of the kidnapper in the white woody station wagon. Once I got behind a house, I stopped. Bent over with my hands on my knees to catch my breath, all I could think of was that little boy. I felt horrible that I was unable to do anything to help. I walked the rest of the way home and couldn't wait to peel the cellophane off my arms and legs. My face was bright-red and I was so thirsty. I tried to erase this from my memory. The guilt. The fear. The experience. What a shitty person. This is when I began to question the concept of "Why do shitty things happen to good people"? I was just a jogger trying to trim some thigh fat. That young boy did not seem like he was excited about finding a new friend and picking her up on the side of the road. Pretty shitty.

I never forgot that day and how helpless I had felt. I hope that little boy made it somehow. I've prayed for him. I've thought about him many times over my life and I questioned why the man who was driving wanted me to hop in the car. What was he going to do with me? The boy? Did he want me to live in a shack with him and the boy so we can pretend to be a family? I had no idea, but I thought the worst. Feeling helpless makes me want to scream. I see this scene in my head often. It makes me want to scream. That hot day comes back to haunt me every once in a while. I am thankful that I survived.

Remember, I had that beyond-real dream of seeing the light body in the long tunnel with the message for me to stay here on Earth as it wasn't yet my time? I hold onto hope, and sometimes I come back to that dream because it seemed important that I know never to give up.

I wondered why so many people wanted to hurt me or others. I knew I wanted to make a difference in other people's lives and help others somehow. I did not ever want to hurt anyone. I was fearful and did not trust many people at that point. I was sensitive and easily hurt by words and actions, and I wished I had someone to talk to about all of my experiences. I read many books and came to understand why people go to church. I knew the difference from right and wrong. I knew how I wanted to be treated by the people I loved and by many strangers, but I wasn't so lucky.

Wendy Zell

Bon Jovi concert 1988

Phillip Pooped in my Pink Patent Leather Purse

High School Prom 1989

Chapter 7:
"If you're a really mean person, you're going to come back as a fly and eat poop."
–Kurt Cobain

FOR SIX MONTHS during high school, I worked at a store called Branden's Home Store. It was a home appliance and furnishings store. This is where I met my dear friend, Peter. I mention him because Peter kept showing up in my life at the weirdest times. When I met Peter, I thought "way too cute, out of my league" and never showed interest in him to avoid getting hurt. He was tall, blonde, and dream-like. Peter and I were both sixteen years old but went to different high schools, so we didn't hang in the same crowds. If I could have created the perfect man, he would have looked exactly like Peter. We were just friends, but Peter would tease me a lot just to see me laugh when we worked together. That made me like him even more, but I couldn't tell him about my crush on him. I stopped working at Branden's to get a job at the mall selling clothes at Units. Peter was my 2nd crush. He was the Peter Pan to my Wendy Darling.

Phillip Pooped in my Pink Patent Leather Purse

While I was sixteen, I fell hard for a guy named Alan who I met on the Fort Lauderdale Strip with my work friends one night while we were cruisin' A1A. He was in town for the summer living with his parents in Boca Raton, but was a student at McGill University in Montreal, Canada, studying to be a lawyer. He was gentle, respectful, kind, sexy, and funny. I was mostly intrigued with his intelligence and worldly knowledge. Alan had very dark hair, dark eyes, a thin body, but looked like a male model. We spent the summer together going to the beach, movies, and dance clubs. I looked forward to rainy days, because he worked as a landscaper with one of his friends. The guys would stop working when it rained, and this heartthrob would call and say he's free for the rainy day. It was a very fun summer!

Alan broke my heart when he left and went back to Montreal to attend university. I received letters from him occasionally and had to look up many of the words he wrote. I needed to define them and understand what he was trying to communicate. His level of vocabulary was far above mine at sixteen, and I became inspired to improve my vocabulary.

During my senior year, no one compared to Alan, so my standards were high again, and I would dump boys left and right after just a few weeks. So I now apologize to all those guys whose heart I broke during my high school years. Not really. You probably deserved it. This was not the end of Alan in my life. We had a connection for over eleven years, on and off, but we lived separate lives. He was my first real crush or love or infatuation, I'm not really sure. He was hard to let go of.

Dad, me, and Mom when I was 16

At seventeen, I graduated from high school with a 3.5 GPA. Right before I graduated from high school, I lost and mourned my Grandma Allen to the angels in heaven. That broke my heart so much more because I adored my grandma and spent a lot of time with her throughout my seventeen years. I have so many memories of her that you can read about in my second book. She made me feel so incredibly special and people don't forget those people who make them feel that special. She spent quality time with me that shaped who I am today.

Phillip Pooped in my Pink Patent Leather Purse

My first car, 1983 Mazda RX7

I drove my own car to graduation that year. This was a very special memory, because I picked up and drove my Grandpa Allen in my silver '83 Mazda RX-7 to the ceremony. During that ride, my grandpa confessed to me that he feels like he's dying of a broken heart. He and my grandma had just celebrated their 58th wedding Anniversary. They bickered often but were a super cute couple.

I began community college studying fashion marketing and merchandising within the next few months. I worked full-time as an assistant manager of a Units clothing store at the Fashion Mall in Plantation, FL and went to school with a full-time schedule. I joined a marketing club and was nominated as an officer, Secretary of DECA, led by the marketing department chair.

One day, that department chair and professor, Dr. Richard Goodwin, asked me to drive him to pick up his antique Corvette that was in the shop. He had been my professor for 3 months and we worked together in the DECA club. It was about a thirty minute drive, but I didn't have to be at work until 4pm that day. He offered me a full tank of gas and a free lunch. I was a broke college student and I respected this man. Dr. Goodwin was my salesmanship professor and he was the staff sponsor for our DECA club. He took our class to see Zig Ziglar speak and was an excellent professor. He was in his 60s, and I was seventeen. After class that morning, we took off in my silver Mazda, and headed to Pompano Beach. Dr. Goodwin changed my life that day. After we picked up his white convertible 69 Corvette, I followed him to his quaint tree-covered house and left my car in his driveway. Dr. Goodwin drove me to a restaurant and said he wanted to talk to me about something important.

I was a little nervous because most men had only seen my outer beauty and did not bother to look within. But not Dr. Goodwin. He took me to a nice place on the beach with white curtains and white cloth napkins. I was not sure what to expect and was curious about what he had to tell me. He complimented me on my intelligence, leadership, integrity, and creativity. He told me that I should reach for higher goals and that he could help me get into any university that I desired. Everyday he said, "It's not what you know, it's who you know that will get you ahead in life." He knew a lot of people in the world of academia. I told Dr. Goodwin that I would think about it.

At that time, now eighteen years old, I was working at the Fashion Mall in Plantation as an Assistant Manager of Units. My friend, Peter, would stop in often just to say hi, since he followed me and got a job at the mall after Branden's. One night, he asked me if I wanted to hang out with him and some of his friends after I got off of work. I was shocked because I always thought Peter was out of my league. I followed him in my car to a small party. After being there for about thirty minutes, Peter asked if he could talk to me outside. I wanted to go home, so I asked him to talk to me as he walked me out to my car. There were other kids there who he went to high school with that I didn't know, so I felt a little out of place.

Phillip Pooped in my Pink Patent Leather Purse

Peter was a gentleman. He told me that there is a girl at the party that likes him, but all he can do is think of me and he didn't know what to do about that. I had no idea that he was going to say that to me. He leaned down and grabbed my face. Peter looked me in my eyes and kissed me. It was a nice, long, gentle kiss. I thought we were just friends, but his flirty ways got me wondering. I wanted more than anything to be with someone like Peter. He was a "10", very handsome, tall, with broad shoulders and nice, strong arms. He danced and I liked that about him! I told him that it would be better for us to be friends. I didn't tell him this, but I was too insecure to have a boyfriend as good looking as Peter. A lot of girls liked him and I didn't blame them, but didn't want the competition. He asked me for a hug goodbye, and he slipped in another kiss. I drove away in shock.

Image © Pinterest

A month later, my best friend, Cindy, and I took a trip up to the University of Florida in Gainesville, a five-hour road trip. She was seeing a guy from our high school named Jim, a student at UF, so we stayed with him and his roommates. Well, that's all it took. I fell in love with one of Jim's roommates and was convinced that I had to go to UF. This was 1989. Gas was ninety-nine cents per gallon. I told Dr. Goodwin that I wanted to transfer to Gator Country as soon as possible, and he told me everything I'd have to do in order to stand out and get accepted. I had to take the SAT a total of three times to get scores high enough. I wasn't giving up. He also recommended that I send in a picture of myself. I chose an Olan Mills pro-shot that was taken during the spring of my senior year of Cindy and me, all decked out in Gator gear. We had big hair and wore all orange and blue that shouted "Make me a Gator!"

Phillip Pooped in my Pink Patent Leather Purse

My college essay was most likely good because I love to write, and Dr. Goodwin wrote me a fantastic recommendation letter that made me look like a rock star. By December of 1989, I was nominated as a Who's Who Among Students in American Junior Colleges and made it into the 1990 book, thanks to Dr. Goodwin. There was a very special ceremony that my parents and I attended. I felt very proud. I even got a new dress.

By April of 1990, I was accepted into the University of Florida as a transfer student. Now I had to break the news to my parents that I applied and got in. I had kept this a secret because my brother was going to art school and I knew they couldn't afford to pay for both of us. Needless to say, my parents were on the fence about me going to UF. My boyfriend, who I wanted to be with, was a Cuban from North Miami, where my dad taught for more than twenty years. I'm sure he thought that my boyfriend was like his slacker students, but that couldn't be further from the truth. Steve was a high school valedictorian, football player, good Catholic boy, and a pre-med student at UF. He had a great family and very nice friends. I was smitten and determined to be with him. Driving those five hours to visit Steve often was hard on both of us. He was a catch and I wasn't going to let him go that easy.

My student ID at UF

August, 1990, I packed up my needed belongings and was ready to start my new life. I was ready to be independent and live on my own away from my family for the first time. I had great roommates, friends, and the best boyfriend I could have ever asked for. Everything was stellar! I was manifesting my dreams. Being on that big campus of the University of Florida made me feel so smart and hopeful for my future. I was unstoppable and had big dreams!!

The first day of classes was so exciting. It was a sunny day riding my bright pink mountain bike up hills to the student union. I was wearing a cute preppy college outfit, my hot pink polo shirt and white jean shorts, tan legs, and my favorite white Keds with no socks. I met my roommate, Amy, there and we saw people talking about a rumor. Amy and I were curious and listened in to those around us. Many students were reading *The Independent Florida Alligator*, the UF school newspaper with shocked faces.

What's going on? Another student gave me a copy of his newspaper and I began reading. Two local college students were murdered in their nearby apartment and found that morning. They were both college girls with brown hair, close to my age, and living a few streets over. Amy and I were scared and shocked, as was the rest of our Gator community in Gainesville, FL.

For the next few days, we continued on as normal as we could, but more murders were happening around us and the gruesome details made everyone fear for their lives. No one could trust anyone. The media thought it was a med school student because he used scalpels. By the end of my first week at UF, there were five murders, all of whom were students who lived within minutes of me and my friends. Students were having massive slumber parties so people would feel safe. One of the victims was a male who tried to fight off the murderer, but he didn't win. His roommate's head was decapitated and placed on the mantle for the police to find. All of the other victims were brunette females and their bodies were all displayed in a disrespectful manner. Nobody was safe. By the end of my first week away at school for the first time, my parents made me come home to South Florida. It was very scary to experience living in a town with a serial killer on the loose. All of us will remember how Danny Rolling made us feel; unsafe, untrusting, and in disbelief. This man will come back as a fly in his next life and eat poop.

The 5 victims and Danny Rolling, Gainesville murderer

I was relieved to be out of Gainesville while they investigated the murders and found the killer, Danny Rollings, a psychopath, who was mad at his ex-wife. My boyfriend, Steve, remained on campus, because he couldn't miss his pre-med classes. My dad insisted on me coming home and driving the five hours, so I did. After two weeks at home missing classes, I was able to convince my parents to let me go back to school at UF. Once they found the murderer and the town was calm again, I wanted to go back. This was the first time I can remember my parents telling me, "I love you!" as I pulled out of our driveway to head back to gator country, and it meant a lot. I didn't know what to think, really. I had always wondered why they hadn't told me sooner. I thought it should be normal to hear those words from my parents, the people raising me. My boyfriend told me often, but hearing it from my parents meant that they cared.

The first couple of years on my own, away at college, I started going to church every Sunday and stayed focused on doing well in school. A friend of mine, Lisa, had me become saved as a Christian in her Baptist church, but I took to the traditions in a Catholic Church and prayed quietly and secretly for peace. My boyfriend, roommates, and I went to Catholic church together every weekend. Within a few months, the UF campus was alive again and full of fun and excitement. Football games, frat parties, etc. ... went on and the fear slowly subsided.

A few months later, I started receiving letters and cards from a man who lived next door to my parents in our hometown of Davie, FL. Terry and his wife lived next door to us for all of my years while I was in high school and they became my parents' best friends. He was very close to my family, was married to my mom's best friend, and was over at our house often. We spent holidays together, but they did not have any children of their own. Terry was a short man, bald, bearded, and always talking about women while boasting bikini pictures of them in his home. I thought that was gross since he was a married man. In the letters, Terry claimed that he was in love with me and couldn't stop thinking about me. I did not feel the same and I was sick by the thought. When I came home for holiday breaks, I kept a job as a hostess at an Italian restaurant that also had a separate bar and nightclub with live entertainment. Terry would show up and drink at the bar while watching me work. He didn't want me to know, but I saw him a few times when he'd go to the bathroom in the same hallway as my hostess stand. I ignored him, but one day, I got up the courage to tell my parents that I was afraid to go home. I told my parents all about Terry and his coming on to me. I sent my parents the letters and cards and told them that he creeps me out while probably undressing me with his eyes. I was nineteen. No thank you! I was afraid to go home for holiday visits because of Terry. I didn't feel comfortable going to my family home anymore, because I knew I'd see him. My parents received my letter to them explaining why I didn't feel comfortable going back home to South Florida. They sent me a flower display with a teddy bear that was delivered to my apartment door since I was five hours away. I called my Mom and she said that my dad was pretty upset. They had a talk with Terry and his wife. He was expected to attend therapy sessions to help him. I'm not sure if it ever helped him, but I kept my distance as often as possible.

My best friend, Cindy, followed me up north and went to the local community college in Gainesville. So did my heart-throb friend, Peter. Remember him? I found this out one night when I was at a really cool bar with Cindy. This is one of those bars where you can buy all different flavors of frozen drinks in icee-looking machines filled with vodka or other liquors that make you sick. Well I was feeling mighty fine after three or four frozen sin drinks that tasted like watermelon or cotton candy. Steve and I were broken up and I was out to meet guys. I saw Peter standing on a bridge near a little lake within the bar property. I couldn't believe my eyes. What is Peter doing here? This guy shows up everywhere I am. I was five hours away from home and had no idea that Peter now lived in my college town. I was twenty, tipsy from the frozen fruit drinks, and in complete shock to see Peter. He insisted on us catching up and going back to his apartment. I threw up the whole way there. Peter had to pull his car over and he stayed with me, held my hair back from getting vomit in it, and gave me napkins from his glove box. He was like Superman, while I was a complete mess. Drunk and throwing up next to this hunk of a friend of mine who told me a couple years prior that he couldn't stop thinking about me. I was so embarrassed, because I wanted to kiss him again like we did almost three years ago. I couldn't do it. Peter insisted that I just lie in his arms and he would just hold me all night. It was heavenly!! When I got up the next morning, I was a wee bit embarrassed about throwing up in front of him, but he didn't seem phased by it at all. Peter laughed as we talked about the night before. He just kissed me on the forehead and I left once I sobered up and could get myself home safely.

Image © Pinterest

Despite the Gainesville Ripper who devastated our town and the letters and stalking from Terry, I had the best four years of my life at the University of Florida. During my time at UF, I finally went to counseling and talked about my past that bothered me. I told Steve and he was more than kind. Steve and I lasted almost three years as a couple while attending UF, but after he graduated, he went off to medical school. I tried to make the long distance work, but I was tempted by frat boys and being in my twenties! Clearly I wasn't ready to settle down and hearts got broken that didn't deserve it. I dated other guys in college but not any who I wanted to marry. As a matter of fact, I did date a Mick for a hot second (about three months) and he was an arrogant turd. He told me that if I married him, I would not work a day in my life. I was not allowed to call him. He could only call me. He was five years older than me and attended UF as a business major, getting his MBA. Mick was tall, very handsome, and intelligent-looking with glasses. Ok, maybe he was a hot nerd, but regardless, that's my type. I told him I wasn't attending UF for my "MRS" degree. I thought this was clever. Mick 3 didn't like that very much. He's the same Mick who questioned if I should be eating a Snickers bar one day. It was my 21st birthday and I could eat whatever I damn well pleased. He sent me a dozen roses to apologize. This wasn't going to be a match. In his big blue eyes, women were to be seen, not heard and this woman doesn't do well with being silenced. Bye, Mick 3.

Graduation Day May 1994

Right before I graduated from UF, I cut my hair very short to look professional. I was now a teacher and wanted to look the part. I was trying to earn some respect and had hoped to be treated like a smart woman with good ideas and a caring heart. I wanted to make a difference and help students who struggled with school and life. I felt bad for people who struggled, because I knew the feeling and I wanted to help. Before I graduated from UF, I invited Steve out to dinner at the Melting Pot in Gainesville. I didn't have the money, but my good friend, Susanne, had a credit card and she told me to treat him to a nice dinner. I invited Steve because I was just about to graduate from University of Florida with summa cum laude, and I was extremely proud of myself. I wanted to thank him for encouraging me to apply to UF and for being the reason that brought me here. Steve and I had a nice evening together talking and eating fondue, but I knew that I hurt him and he'd never be able to see me in the same light. I had to walk away with my tail between my legs and say goodbye to this one, too. I had to find some closure before I moved on and began my life in South Florida. Steve was so good to me when we were together. He deserved to be very happy and successful. I had to close this chapter in my book, but I will always feel grateful for his love and care for the many years I enjoyed it. I guess it just wasn't meant to be. I still had a lot to learn.

Phillip Pooped in my Pink Patent Leather Purse

Chapter 8:
Have a Nice Poop!

SINCE I MOVED home in May of 1994 after graduation and school didn't begin until August, I started a job as Assistant Manager of a Gymboree children's clothing store to make money that summer. My manager and friend, Stacy, introduced me to Mick 4, her cousin visiting from Buffalo, NY. This one taught me how to rollerblade, he introduced me to new music, and made an impression on me because he was honest, witty, intelligent, and real. We dated that summer while Mick 4 was in FL, but he had to return to Buffalo in August where he was still in university studying quantum physics or something of that nature. He was extremely intelligent and had very unique ideas and philosophies about the world we live in, so I of course was intrigued. I had already believed in reincarnation and coming back to make old relationships better, but I knew nothing of quantum physics. I liked being around him. He was peaceful and natural. Mick 4 believed that there are parallel universes happening at the same time we are functioning and living on earth. I wanted to know more. He tried explaining to me that there are so many levels of energy and we are living in a physical world, but some you cannot see. We decided to have a long distance relationship even though he was apprehensive and honest about the possibility of it being difficult. He was a realist.

I bought a plane ticket with my own teaching money and went to visit Mick 4 in Buffalo, NY during the fall of that year. He wanted me to take a trip with him to Lake Placid. It was a very romantic town with horse drawn carriages along the beautiful lake. One day, we hiked Mount Marcy, the tallest mountain in the Adirondack mountains of New York. The whole journey took a total of thirteen hours from the bottom to the top, and then back down (which was more challenging than you'd think) to the bottom. It was late October and the leaves were just amazing to me, because I lived in Florida and we did not have such foliage. Mick 4 laughed at me because all of his friends were nature hippies and here I was with my white tennis shoes and long nails with red nail polish ready to climb a huge mountain. I thought climbing that big mountain and making it all the way down without breaking something was a big deal to me. It was thirteen hours with only granola bars to eat. This was total-hippie-life and I loved it. It's too bad that such an exciting adventure and cool memory had to end with a guy who dumped me over the phone that Christmas Eve and told me he wasn't coming to fly down to see me for Christmas. That was the end of that Mick. I should have learned by now that anyone by the name of Mick would be bad news for me. I cried that night on Christmas Eve, but I moved on. I remember my cousins were here celebrating with our family, so they all made me feel better.

My family trying to cheer me up on 12/24

At twenty-two, I started teaching students with a variety of exceptional needs in a middle school in Palm Beach County. It was hard work. I was inexperienced, new, and challenged daily. My motto was "work hard, play hard". I was confident in myself as a teacher even though I was being called every name in the book by my emotionally impaired students and had my classroom totalled weekly whenever one of them got angry. I enjoyed my job most of the time, because the people I worked with were awesome human beings. But the kids were tough. It took a lot of effort to manage behavior and get kids to learn and be happy. I still felt like a kid myself trying to figure out this crazy thing we call life. I loved my job and working with these kids. They taught me so much. I have plans to write my third memoir that will include stories of my experiences as a special education teacher in Florida and Michigan.

Being with my friends, especially Carrie, helped me get over my lost loves and broken hearts. We spent three to four nights per week dancing at clubs and were in great shape. One night, we were dancing at Baja Beach Club and I couldn't believe my eyes. I saw Peter, my hunk friend.

There he was dressed in a bow tie and short Jean shorts allowing women to do body shots off of his tan, muscular, hairless chest. He jumped up on the bar and rested on his knees leaning back so the drunk girls could lick the whipped cream off of his chest before getting his shorts all creamy. They threw money at him and waited for him to put more whipped cream in their mouths. I was jealous. I wish I had the nerve to do that to Peter. I was too shy and didn't do things like that. He didn't see me watching him as he worked the counter. The club was dark, loud, and filled with beautiful women. Once I built up the nerve, I said hi to Peter and he seemed really excited to see me and a little embarrassed. I smiled and told him that it's okay. I confessed that I was modeling bikinis at the Sands Marina and Hotel on Saturdays for my friend who owned a bikini shop. We both laughed and he had to go back to work. The bikini model days were fun, but somewhat demeaning. I did not care to have my body stared at like a piece of meat.

Phillip Pooped in my Pink Patent Leather Purse

Me and Carrie 1995

About six months later, I was in my car driving my garbage to the dumpsters in my apartment complex. Guess who pulled up right behind me? Yep. Peter! He now lived in my apartment complex in Coconut Creek, FL. It was so weird seeing him at the dumpster. I keep running into this guy all over Florida, but nothing comes of it. We had always just remained friends but there was a deep level of respect and self-control. The chemistry and attraction were there, but timing was always off. I wasn't going to press the issue or force anything.

Another year rolls by, and I read an article in the newspaper that told me Peter Cook was killed in a car accident. My heart stopped, and I couldn't believe it. That was my Peter!! I was incredibly saddened by Peter's death. I did not know any of Peter's friends because we went to different high schools, so I was lucky to have seen the article in the paper. I had always wondered if he was going to be there for me in the end, but now that he was dead, I had to hope for another knight in shining armor. Peter made me feel safe. I didn't trust many people, especially men. I knew I wouldn't keep running into Peter anymore. This made me sad. I was going to miss the mystery and wonder of "what if". I was so sad that another amazing soul was taken from this planet too young. He was inspiring to me, because Peter was always so kind and gentle with me, and he never made me feel like a piece of meat. Our attraction for each other was strong, but we never had sex.

Phillip Pooped in my Pink Patent Leather Purse

    I can't help but wonder if those who passed before me; Todd, Peter, and my grandmothers, are watching over me and rooting for me from the angelic sidelines. Sometimes when I get really lonely, I remember their genuine love and interest in me and everything seems all better.

Chapter 9: Fancy Shit

MY BEAUTIFUL BLONDE friend, Carrie, and I enjoyed the Fort Lauderdale nightlife in our twenties! It was the 90s and the music was underappreciated. We frequented a variety of bars and nightclubs along A1A and US1, all hotspots for celebrities and wealthy people who like to dance and party. Carrie and I dressed to impress every night in cocktail dresses and we danced on top of speakers when the DJ played our songs! We met so many people and had a lot of crazy adventures. We took many road trips to Key West, Ybor City in Tampa, and Orlando to enjoy the nightlife, as well.

    I dated several guys who were wealthy, but there were some uncomfortable feelings when I was around them. I did not feel like I fit in. I drove in Porsches, Mercedes, and BMWs on dates to expensive restaurants, polo matches in West Palm Beach, and amazing concerts. My favorite was a date with a man named Bruce, to a Van Halen concert in Miami and dinner in South Beach. He drove a very fast red Acura NSX. On our ride to Miami, he opens up his glovebox and pulls out 2 champagne glasses and a bottle of expensive bubbly. He was ten years older than me, but he knew how to treat a lady. We took a walk on the beach in Miami after dinner and I was treated with respect. I did not continue to see this man, because I felt uncomfortable with the age difference. He was a successful UF Grad, like me, so we had this in common, but not much else.

Phillip Pooped in my Pink Patent Leather Purse

Me at 24 and my pup, Ginger

    I met Brad, my fancy golfer boyfriend, when I was twenty-four. There was this blonde babe in his black Jeep Wrangler, all tan with his collared shirt and racoon eyes from wearing sunglasses all day, that I had a hard time resisting. Brad in his Jeep, assertively pulled into the spot I was trying to get at a Big Daddy's Lounge in Boca Raton, FL, one evening when I went out with friends. Once I was in the bar I let him know that he took my spot that I was waiting for, and I bummed a cigarette off of him. He bought me a Corona and we got to know each other a little better. I told him that I was a teacher and he said that we have something in common. He explained that he is a golf instructor at the Boca Raton Country Club, so I was drawn in immediately. His eyes were light blue, like a bright sky and his smile was huge. Brad was a heartbreaker. I could tell. But, I went out with him anyway. For the first year, things were amazing between us. I found out that he was really just the cart and bag guy at the fancy country club in the golf shop, but every once in a while, he would give someone lessons. So, there were more red flags…a guy who lies to impress a girl and makes her think that he is better than he really is. Brad was an awesome golfer, with a 5 or 7 handicap. He stood tall, perfectly thin, tan, sexy, and had a great swing. Brad had a smile that everyone fell in love with. He smiled a huge grin, but his eyes smiled with his lips and it was so tempting. I was looking my best when I met him. I had been modeling bikinis in a poolside fashion show on the weekends, so I kept in shape and tanned often. I was swept away into his world of being with his fancy friends. Even though Brad was only the cart guy at the fancy club, all of his friends were wealthy club members who wanted to help Brad become a successful PGA tour member. "It's not what you know, It's WHO you know" that rang in my ears, so I was glad that Brad had big dreams, even though he didn't go to school to study. Brad's fancy friends took us out to these big dinners with a dozen or so people, several bottles of red wine on the table, escargot, prime rib, filet mignon, lobster, crab legs, and champagne toasts. One of the rich couples would pay for everyone at the table. Brad and I never paid for these elaborate dinners. We would all smoke big cigars and drink red wine or Brandy after dinner. Sometimes they would hold the dark dance club open for us after dinner and we danced the night away. I loved that Brad would get up and dance with me. He would even make up funny dances, like the "scoop and dig" and he was silly enough to show off how well he could do the "sprinkler". Brad and I had a lot of fun and we had a good physical relationship during the first year. We decided to get an apartment together and move in with one another. We were excited to make this new step and we shopped for new furniture to make it look perfect for us. Brad and I had a cute 2-bedroom 2-bath apartment in Boca Raton, FL, and we had two dogs together; Ginger and Emmitt. We played house every day, and every night we'd crack open a bottle of red wine and drink several glasses out on our balcony overlooking the stars and green palm trees. Brad and I had the best talks. We shared our hopes and dreams and we never argued out on that balcony. He was my best friend and I trusted him, because we had a special bond.

Boca Raton Resort and Golf Country Club

One day, Brad came home from the country club all excited with good news. As we toasted to his news out on the balcony, Brad explained that there are a few golfers who would like to sponsor him to play on the PGA tour. Brad went for it and practiced golfing as much as possible, continued our fancy dinners with his sponsors and their wives who never really warmed up to me. I never figured that out. Perhaps it was because I was the only one who had a full time job and had to work to survive, versus being dependent upon their husbands to get the latest fashions, hair, and nail trends. Brad started the tour and I even got to ride in the golf cart with him at several of his events. I enjoyed being by his side and watching him thrive. It was thrilling and I was very proud of him. Sadly, though, one early morning, I got a call from Brad that he was in a bad accident and he broke some bones in his back and ribs. Brad and one of his sponsors went out drinking and kept drinking, until they were too drunk to drive. Brad drove the 2-seater red Mercedes around town that night and hit a pole and passed out. Brad had to drop out of the PGA tour and rest in our home for a while until he was healed. He was out of a job and I took over paying all of the bills. Following this, Brad decided to become a stock broker, because his fancy friends could give him a foot into a local firm.

So many changes in this man's life in such a short time dating him and now here I am supporting him. Stock brokers make no money for the first year, so I allowed him to just live in the home while making no income. I was a fool and I was getting frustrated that I was paying all of the bills for the apartment, the furniture payments, cable, groceries, etc. … In addition, his ego was beginning to grow since being on the PGA tour, so he was much more ballsy with what he said to women, even my friends. Brad asked one of my close friends, who had just gotten a boob job, if he could see her boobs after her surgery. I didn't think this was cool, but he sure got mad when I stood up for myself and explained that he crossed a line. Another time, one of his friends got a new girlfriend and she came to our house one night after getting a new tattoo. I believe it was in a spot where only lovers would see it, close to her panties. He asked her to take him into the bathroom and show him her tattoo. When I came down the stairs and heard them in the bathroom giggling while her pants were down around her knees and you could clearly see her panties and her new tattoo. I was hurt and that was twice now that my boyfriend asked two other women I knew to go beyond what I would do, as deemed appropriate. I thought this was pretty shitty.

Then, one night, after coming home really late from a night out with his fancy friends, I questioned why his hair was wet and he was drunk and so late. He told me a group of them went skinny dipping in the pool. I was not included. I did not know what really happened. Brad had issues with having to quit the PGA tour. It threw his dreams out the window. He went after another dream of trying to be a successful stock broker and asking his fancy friends to invest in him. Even though this would take years to begin making a decent income, Brad was determined to impress these friends with all stakes in. I put my foot down and stood up for myself when I thought he crossed the line with other women or with his friends. He would get angry at me and act like he was God's gift to this world. His fancy friends must be building up his ego. One afternoon, he came home all drunk and told me that he wasn't in love with me anymore. He packed up his things and left me with our apartment, furniture, two dogs, and everything but his clothes and clubs.

Brad had some regrets and reached out to win me back a couple of times after he realized that he made a big mistake. I was there for him when he lied, fell, succeeded, and was so broke he didn't know where his next meal would come from. But I wasn't someone who lived this fancy lifestyle, had the best of everything, or even had the most top-designer clothes. I did what I could on my teacher salary and I'm sorry that I spoke my mind and didn't let you think it was okay to undress all of my friends with your eyes. I was hurt by him, but mostly because I gave so much and was not treated with the respect I thought was earned.

After Brad, I rented out the other bedroom in the apartment until the lease was up, and then I moved into a 1-bedroom that backed up to the volleyball courts in a different apartment complex further west. Brad's sister, Stephanie, and I remained friends so I was aware of how he was living his life. Let's just say, I'm glad I didn't stick around and fall for anymore of his lies or allow him to depend on me financially anymore.

One night, months later, Stephanie was celebrating her divorce and we went to a bar to meet up with some friends. Carrie and Dawn were with me that night, also. It was a packed bar called Rush Street on Las Olas Blvd in Downtown Fort Lauderdale. They were serving drinks in little plastic cups and they all tasted watered down by the time each drink passed its way through four hands just to get to its owner. After four tiny Rum and Cokes, all watered down, I was crashing on the dance floor and falling down like my legs had no feeling in them. I was dancing with a tall handsome guy named Leif, that I had a major crush on, and he brought me to my friends. He told them I kept falling down. I knew it wasn't the alcohol. I did not feel drunk at all. Each drink was weak and watered down. Thank God for Leif and his respect. Thank you for taking me to my friends and not taking advantage of me. I kept running away from my friends and tried running into the street to find my car. I remember wanting to go home but it wasn't even that late. My friends had no idea what had happened to me and they thought I was really drunk. "I think someone slipped a roofie in my drink!", I told my friend Stephanie when I woke up the next morning and wondered how I got home and why she was at my apartment. There were poppy seeds all over my white counters in the kitchen and she told me that I insisted on having an everything bagel with scrambled eggs and salsa at midnight. She thought it was weird, because I blacked out and hadn't remembered the past three hours of the night. She told me the whole story and I had zero recollection of doing anything she said I did. All I have to say is that I am so thankful that I was with good friends that night. I was twenty-six and still had more life to live. Roofies were all the rage then. Girls were being roofied and raped never to be seen again in our area, so I considered myself lucky!

Phillip Pooped in my Pink Patent Leather Purse

Chapter 10:

Flush it down...

WHEN I WAS twenty-seven in 1999, I met my son's father. This ended my dance club and dating rich guys phase while in my twenties. My first husband was not rich and did not dance. He was a very serious business guy with a goofy side who appeared to have his shit together. He had a nicely decorated condo in Deerfield Beach, two cars, and jet skis for us to enjoy on the weekends. He felt like independence and freedom. I was vulnerable and tired of being treated like a stupid blonde by guys I met in clubs or bars. Right before I met Mick, I dyed my hair a purplish red with hopes that a man would take me seriously. I met this one when online dating first became a popular thing to do in the late nineties. Most people had a home computer by this time, so online dating was new and mysterious. My ex-husband is Mick 5. I will not go into too much detail about this relationship because it's my son's father. However, it was not easy, but we remain friends to this day. When I met my son's father, I was immediately attracted to his height of 6'4", slender build, soft blue eyes, and nice dark hair. We had serious conversations and we both had big dreams.

A few months after I met Mick 5, my mother decided to leave my father and begin a new life. My parents were living about thirty minutes away and we spent a lot of time together, because I enjoyed their company. One day, my dad asked me to come over so he could talk to me. He was in shock and tried to show me all of the pictures he found to prove that my mom is a lesbian. I couldn't look at the pictures, and instead I chose to look away. I didn't want it to be how I remember my mom. She is my mom and regardless of who she is with, I don't want to know what she is doing sexually. My mom left my dad and moved in with her girlfriend, a teacher leader at her school. Eventually, months later, she admitted to me that she was a lesbian, but it was really hard for my mom to do that. She was married to my dad for thirty-three years. They were a cute couple, but it was obvious that they didn't have a strong connection. I never heard I-love-you's and never really witnessed much cuddling or positive vibes. It was all so confusing for me.

Dealing with my parents' divorce was very hard on me. I clung to Mick 5 because he had a nice home and told me that he would take care of me. I had my first panic attack in my apartment after I found out about my mom. The shock was wearing off that she was a lesbian and I began worrying about the judgement of others. This was 1999 when coming out of the closet was beginning to be more popular, but I never expected my own mom to make that choice to come out. The anxiety started spiraling and I only had negative thoughts. I couldn't stop thinking about all of the worst scenarios, facing my friends and co-workers again. I couldn't even imagine how my mom must have felt. I curled up in the corner of my bedroom and balled my eyes out, hyperventilating, rolling back and forth trying to soothe myself, trying to tell myself that everything was going to be okay. I just couldn't get out of that negativity well. The tears kept coming. It felt like they would never end. I lit a white candle thinking it would help and it did a little bit, but I couldn't help but think about how I never would have guessed that my parents would divorce. It was a shock to me and more so because I felt like a fool for not knowing all this time. I knew Mick 5 didn't treat me the way I wanted to be treated, but he was all I had then. I was so weak, sad, and confused.

I couldn't do it. I quit my job as a teacher to middle school students with special needs after two weeks into my 6th school year in Boca Raton, FL. I disappeared from my close friends and I just wanted to be by myself. I wanted to run and hide and maybe the pain would go away.

I needed a job, so I became a manager of the ladies-only fitness center where I worked out in Boca Raton, FL. I moved in with Mick 5 and still wasn't happy in that relationship, but I needed a place to live and someone by my side. We rang in the millennium together with close friends that New Year's Eve. I had these recurring thoughts for years that I would marry the man I spent New Year's Eve with in 1999/2000. Two months later, Mick 5 was offered a job and a transfer within his company to a small town in Michigan named Plymouth. I had never been there, and I imagined it would be farmland with a few grocery stores within the town. We broke up while he started his new life in Michigan. I needed to be there for my dad, because he was hurting deeply from my parents separation and the shocking news about my mom.

While I was a manager of the gym, I worked out every day and enjoyed meeting new people. One day, I sold a 3-year gym membership to a woman named Sherri, another angel who will be in my second book. She offered me a different job and became my only friend, since I had pushed all others away. Sherri was a single woman with a son she adored, a beautiful home, and a successful career. She took me under her wing while she and I traveled all over the state of Florida selling workout, dance, and swim wear to sporting goods stores, dance studios, fitness centers, and country clubs in the finest areas. I loved traveling with Sherri because we always sang in the car (Les Misérables, London Version) and she had so much wisdom to share since she was about twenty years my elder. She was and still is a beautiful woman on the inside and out. I trained and worked with lovely Sherri selling Marika, Danskin, and Nike Swimwear for nearly 4 months, until it dawned on me that in order to be happy, it was time to leave Florida and start fresh. I wanted to escape the pain and the reality of my life.

I was working for Sherri, but traveling on my own one week, and I was fed up with the Florida traffic, heat, and only having one friend left nearby. I felt lonely and wanted a better life. As I was driving down the turnpike I played a game with myself. I noticed a lot of cars passing me from other states as I admired license plates. I wondered what it would be like to live somewhere other than Florida. Maybe that's what I needed - a brand new start. First, I saw Colorado and wondered what it would be like to live in the beautiful mountains. My friend, Kevin, lived there and I always thought he was cool for being so brave and moving away. Maybe I'll move to Colorado. Then I saw Georgia and thought Atlanta might be a great place to start over in my twenties. But I saw more Michigan license plates than any other, and I wondered if it was all farmland like I imagined. I hadn't heard from Mick 5 in over a month so I didn't take that tug too seriously. It was now March of 2000. The new millennium was here and I was ready to be brave and leave Florida once and for all. I knew I had to do it for myself.

That evening, I came home and checked my email on my laptop. We didn't yet have cell phones that told us we have an email, so I was unaware until I made it home. I was living with my dad since Mick 5 moved to Michigan. I had been traveling all day by car and finally opened up my email to read them. Mick 5 sent me an email that afternoon around the same time I was thinking about moving out of FL. His words on the screen asked me if I would move to Michigan, because he thought I would love it there. I thought it was a sign since I had thought all day about leaving, and I saw so many Michigan plates. He was lonely and wanted to give us another chance. I took my dad to Arby's that night and told him the news. "I'm moving to Michigan, dad. I decided today that it's best for me to get out of Florida. There is pain in my heart wherever I go and I just want to get away from all of the reminders." I told him that I was giving Mick 5 another chance and moving with him in two weeks when he comes back to FL to close on his condo.

My dad was pretty upset and I felt guilty. I just couldn't bear the pain. My parents' divorce affected me more than I realized. I just wanted to run from the memories and go somewhere new. As painful as this was, to just pack up and leave my whole Florida life behind, I believe it was the right thing to do. I knew this decision would hurt my parents, but I had to attempt to take care of myself.

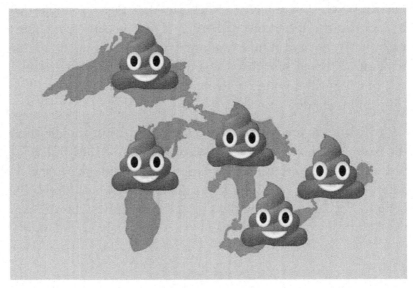

Image © Shutterstock

Chapter 11: I Just Can't Get Away from this Shit!

IT DOESN'T MATTER where I go, the perverts seem to follow me. I moved to Michigan in late April, 2000. I was ready to start my life over! Mick 5 and I lived in an apartment in a normal suburban area, despite my thoughts of it being merely farmland and horses. Michigan is very pretty, clean, and green.

One day after going to a job interview, dressed in a long brown skirt, knee high brown boots, and a long sleeved tan turtleneck, I decided to check out the local bookstore in a strip mall. I wanted some new books about the area, maps for hiking, etc. I grabbed a stack to review and sat in a circle group of nice padded fabric chairs for readers. The coffee shop scents carried over and it made me want a hot beverage, but I didn't want to lose my seat. While I sat there reading, I was approached by an older man in a grey suit. He sat down next to me and asked me what I was reading and if I went to the bookstore often. He was about thirty years older than me and smelled like he just drank a bottle of wine, so I tried to ignore him. I nodded a couple of times to look like I was only interested in my reading. He continued to talk to me in a strange accent. "You're a very sexy woman. I would like to get you naked and take you home with me tonight." That's it. I jumped up and told him that he was a pervert. Then, I walked over to find someone who worked at the bookstore near a computer and I explained what had just happened. The man wasn't sitting there by the time we returned. I asked the store clerk to walk me out to my car because I was afraid he was going to be out there looking for me. The nice young man agreed and walked me towards my car. We both saw the older man in the parking lot walking up and down the aisles. It was nearly dusk, but the street lights were on so we could see him clearly. The young man yelled at him to leave or he will have to call the police. He ran. As I approached my car, the clerk told me to get in and drive away while he kept his eye on the pervert. I was thankful that I asked for help and for his kindness.

I drove away and didn't look back. A woman isn't even safe in a bookstore in a small suburban town in Michigan. I wonder what that man was thinking. There seems to be little respect for women everywhere I go. I guess there are two kinds of women. The ones who want the attention and the ones who don't. I just wonder why a man thinks that he can pick up a woman in a bookstore and take her home to have sex. Is there no respect for women? Why are we always looked at like a piece of meat? Self-control, please, gentlemen.

A week later, in our Northville apartment, while looking for some papers in our file cabinet to get information for job applications, I came across a few porno magazines that I know I did not buy. I confronted Mick and he eventually got rid of them. I created a resume and portfolio of my Florida teaching years, and I found a teaching job about fifteen minutes from my MI apartment. I had several interviews and I was looking forward to working with children again. My principal was a sweet man who was so kind to the elementary students. I began teaching elementary aged students with disabilities and challenges. The staff, parents, and students were cool, and I loved my new job. I met some new friends on this staff that I still have to this day.

Mick 5 and I bought a new house in Plymouth, MI with a pool, in a cute neighborhood, and within walking distance to downtown with shops and restaurants. We had a dog and a cat and what seemed to be a great life. I made amends with my Florida friends and I missed them very much. I seemed a little lost living in Michigan without them. I only knew Mick 5 from Florida and it became lonely. The holidays were hard. My brother had moved to Arizona and later California, so I rarely saw him or his wife. My mom was in Florida, and my dad moved to Chicago to get away from our family home and all of his memories that I'm sure were painful for him, as well.

All of our family albums from vacations over the years were purged in the trash because the memories were too difficult for my parents to bear and hold onto. Several years later, my dad sent me a shoebox with some of the photographs of me over the years growing up. I was appreciative of them because I have so few.

Wendy Zell

Our house in Plymouth, Michigan

Mick 5 and I got engaged in July that summer because it was what he promised my dad he would do before I moved to Michigan. Mick is a devout Catholic and we decided to get married in a Catholic church. I decided to join the RCIA (Rite of Christian Initiation for Adults) Program to gain knowledge, wisdom, prayer, and my confirmation before marrying Mick 5. We thought that going to church would make us better people. I enjoyed the music and the sermons, but not the guilt. We found a church with a funny down-to-earth younger priest in a nice, safe neighborhood. Mick 5 and I enjoyed Father Jim's Sunday sermons and many of the other parishioners admired, became inspired by, and loved him. Mick 5 and I had an interview with him explaining why we wanted me to go through the RCIA Program (Rite of Christian Initiation for Adults). I explained that my parents had me baptized in a Catholic Church, but they only took my brother to CCD classes as a kid and he got his First Holy Communion and Confirmation. This is what I was hoping to accomplish, because I wanted to learn more about my faith and be able to take communion bread in church every Sunday. Father Jim explained that Mick 5 and I would have to go through premarital counseling with him prior to him marrying us in this church. We understood and agreed, as this is standard practice in many churches. In the meantime, Father Jim said he would set me up with a sponsor and I could join the RCIA Program. He told Mick 5 and me that he would want to meet with each of us individually for counseling sessions before we meet together.

Father Jim met with Mick 5 first, then I had an hour-long session with him the following evening. He asked me a few questions, then told me that he doesn't think I should marry Mick. He thinks I am a very beautiful smart woman and could do better than him. Father Jim went on to tell me that Mick 5 was marrying me for the wrong reasons. I have no clue what they discussed, but I was being persuaded to make a change I wasn't ready for. I explained that he is the only person I really know here in Michigan and I think he will get better in time. I let Father Jim know that I was lonely because I had just moved here from Florida. He told me that he would like to be my new best friend. I didn't know what to think of that. I wasn't very pure and couldn't imagine being buds with a Catholic Priest. I listened to him, though, because I thought he had my best interests in mind.

My dog, Ginger, and I moved out of our cute house in Plymouth and found a room to rent in a house in Royal Oak, MI that I shared with two medical students in residency. They were really nice guys who had girlfriends and were rarely ever home. I felt safe and secure living in the basement with a couch, tv, bed, and a silver chrome rack for my clothes. My roommates introduced me to some really nice people and we would go out and enjoy the nightlife and breweries in Royal Oak.

Chapter 12:
Holy Crap!

MEANWHILE, I WAS still attending RCIA weekly meetings and Sunday mass. Father Jim assigned his secretary, Victoria, to be my mentor through the RCIA process. Each week, he would pick me out of the crowd, sit down with me at my table, and ask how I was doing. One evening after class, he invited me out to dinner at a local Macaroni Grill and he shared some intimate secrets with me over some Chianti. Father Jim took off his clerical clothing and dressed in a button down shirt, sweater vest, and black pants. He had an attractive face and looked to be about 36 years old, but he was shorter than me and had lost most of his hair. I was not physically attracted to him, but he told me often that he thought I was beautiful. While at dinner, sipping bold red wine, Father Jim confessed to being in love before and engaged to be married. He broke off the engagement because he felt a calling to be a priest and felt connected to the church. He shared that being a priest is lonely and he appreciated my friendship. Father Jim was so adored and respected at the church I joined. I couldn't imagine him feeling lonely, but I could also see his point because he goes to bed alone every night. I didn't feel sorry for him though, because becoming a priest in a Catholic church meant that you give up marrying anyone else, as you have committed to marrying the church. If he was having second thoughts, then I didn't want to carry that burden. He seemed to be in a state of confusion and wanted confirmation from me that he is making the right choice. I barely knew this man. His secretary was my sponsor and she let me know that Father Jim asks questions about me often. I wasn't sure what to think about that. I started to wonder if Father Jim was hitting on me in some way and it made me a bit uncomfortable.

We talked about the New York Twin Towers in September and how I felt so alone that day. I told him the only person who called me on 9/11 was my dad. I lived in Michigan with no family but I stayed because of my career and rise in income. Father Jim asked me to go golfing. He asked me to go to his sister's house for Thanksgiving and told me that he told his sister all about me. He would call me on the phone and want to talk in the evenings. I was not interested in anything other than friendship from him and perhaps some spiritual guidance. I tried to make that clear by telling him the true stories of going out on dates with other guys. It didn't seem to faze him.

One evening after RCIA class in November, 2001, Father Jim invited me back to his living quarters at the church, the rectory, for a beer and a chat. I agreed while curiously thinking that it would

Phillip Pooped in my Pink Patent Leather Purse

be cool to see where the priest lives. I followed him there and were greeted by his dog, Brenda, a golden Labrador, at the door with her tail wagging. She followed me into the living area where I found a spot on the couch. Father Jim lit some white candles and went to the fridge for two beers. He came back with them, handed me a beer, and sat down next to me on the couch. His dog, Brenda, stayed right next to my side while I enjoyed petting her head, ears, and golden fur. She was very sweet. Father Jim said, "Brenda, you don't know how lucky you are to be touched by a beautiful woman." He went on to tell me that no one wants to hug the priest. He said that most people shake his hand and he gets little affection. Father Jim shared how lonely he was and then he put his hand on my knee, rubbed my thigh, and I jumped up. I put my single-sipped beer down, and told him that I forgot that I had to be somewhere and left. It was so awkward. I walked out quickly, got into my car and drove back to my apartment. I emailed his secretary explaining that I wanted to drop out of RCIA at this church, because I was given a little too much attention by Father Jim. She responded that she wasn't surprised, because he has several lady friends that he invites back to the rectory. Then, she confessed that he specifically asked her to be my sponsor through RCIA so she could give him more information about me. I left this church and never went back. I did not give up on my faith and continued my journey as a Catholic for many years.

A week later, I received a phone call from Mick 5 asking me out to dinner and suite seats to a Red Wings game. I was hurt by Father Jim. Maybe betrayal is a better word. I went out with Mick 5 on that date and we had a very fun time. I felt lonely after 9/11/2001 and desired to know my life's purpose. Mick 5 was reaching out and I took the bait. He convinced me he would make some changes for us to move forward and I believed him.

We got engaged within a few weeks and were married on 2/16/2002. It was a small wedding with only twelve people, including Mick and me. It was in a little wedding chapel that was elegant, quick, and lovely. No dancing, no music, just dinner after the ceremony at a local restaurant. It felt right at the moment, but it was not an easy marriage. I was thirty-one and wanted to settle down and have children. I loved the little kids at my job, so I desperately desired to become a mom. I felt alone here in Michigan, with only a few friends, and I yearned to feel whole and complete. I wanted a happy family. I started reading books about how to get pregnant, spoke with my doctors, friends, and chiropractor. My body needed folic acid, so I made sure to take my vitamins and eat well. My ob-gyn told me that 30 year-olds aren't as fertile as 23-year-olds, and it can take longer for the sperm to break through the cervix and fertilize the egg, so I should be patient. It became a chore to us and wasn't fun anymore. Mick 5 and I went to church every Sunday. I prayed for me to get pregnant because all I wanted was a happy family. I had so much love to give and so many ideas about raising children. Back when I was sixteen, I wrote in my high school Senior Book that I wanted three children. At this point, I would have felt lucky to have one.

After a year of trying to get pregnant, Mick 5 and I decided to have me enter the RCIA classes at our new church. For a year, Mick 5 was my sponsor and we went to weekly meetings to help me find faith and attain my Holy Communion and Confirmation through the Catholic church.

During this journey, I found a place that I could worship and pray for my heart's desires. I was happy to go to church with my husband. We met many other couples with similar struggles. We continued to try and have a child, but my body wasn't having it.

Our RCIA experience gave us many opportunities to be a part of the community by giving back to others and serving those less fortunate. One day, there was a group of twenty of us who made sandwiches and served the homeless in Detroit. Another day, we worked in a soup kitchen in Detroit serving hot meals to the

Phillip Pooped in my Pink Patent Leather Purse

homeless or less fortunate. I enjoyed making other people feel happy and cared about. My desire to be a mom did not go away.

During this time, I would pray to God, Jesus, and all of the Angels and Saints that would take the time to hear me. I would close my eyes and try to connect with the divine. I prayed with feeling, emotion, and desperation for my soul to have what I yearned for so deeply. It was like my life would not be complete without having a child, this child, who I already knew and felt connected to. I had an overwhelming sense of hope and wasn't going to give up.

Mick 5 and I went to see a fertility specialist, but there was nothing wrong with either of us and we just needed to wait and keep trying. I would cry when I got my monthly cycle. For many months, I thought I was pregnant because my mind wanted it so badly, my boobs hurt so bad, and I'd notice mild changes to my body. But, still no luck, after two years. A friend of mine told me that a friend of hers who was having a hard time conceiving a child, went out and bought her dream car, then a month later, she became pregnant. So, I went to the local BMW dealer and leased a silver BMW sedan with a sunroof. It was a beautiful, fast car to drive, but it didn't replace having a child.

Me and my BMW 2003

Me on a trip to Florida 2003, before I was a mom

Phillip Pooped in my Pink Patent Leather Purse

Soon after, Mick 5 and I decided to have a Solemnization Ceremony in our church to validate our marriage by the Catholic church. In February 2004, we were recognized in front of fifty of our closest family and friends and prayed for by the church. The Deacon who spoke at our ceremony knew us through RCIA and made the focus of his sermon and prayers on creating children through this partnership. I wore a pretty, soft yellow-a-lined dress and Mick 5 wore a suit with a matching tie. We celebrated in our church basement with a beautiful cake and champagne. There were gold and white balloons decorating the room. At the end of the party, Mick 5 and I went outside and sent the balloons up into the sky with our wishes to have a child together. It was cold, but it was lovely. I felt so much love this day, and I'll never forget how many people were there for us, adding their prayers for us to have a child.

Three weeks later, I found out I was pregnant!!! I had never wanted something so badly before, and I couldn't believe how fast my prayers were answered. I cherished this little bean inside my body and I was so thankful for this opportunity to become a mom. Everyone we knew could not believe it when I told them I was pregnant around seven weeks. Once we found out that we were having a boy, we immediately went to Babies R Us and shopped for little boy clothes. It was an exciting time in my life. I had a good job working with elementary students and a cute home in Downtown Plymouth. Mick 5 and I decided that we would need a bigger house with a child on the way, so we put our small house up for sale. I loved the neighborhood we lived in because it was walking distance to our beautiful downtown area with shops, restaurants, parks, and a big fountain where everyone goes to get their pictures taken. All of the homes in the Plymouth neighborhood had nice yards and people took pride in caring for them. I loved walking from our house to downtown when I was pregnant with my baby boy, almost every day. He seemed to enjoy me keeping active. I put on a total of fifty pounds when I was pregnant and I was big, so the exercise was certainly welcome. I would walk about a mile and a half to Panera and get a bread bowl with broccoli cheese soup and green tea. My baby wanted cheese, bread, crackers, milkshakes, and hamburgers! Give me a salad and it will end up in the garbage can, because my baby didn't want anything to do with raw fruits or veggies. I lived on my prenatal vitamins to give him what he needed. My body just stored the fat.

My Teacher picture 2004

Selling our home was stressful, because we expected it to sell quickly, and the market wasn't biting as fast as we had hoped. During my fourth month of pregnancy, Mick 5 and I picked out a house about twenty minutes away, closer to the country roads, less people, less traffic, but more money, square footage, and space. We were excited to pick out everything for our new home, but knowing that we had deadlines to sell our other home first, made it incredibly stressful. Mick 5 and I found ourselves fighting over the stress in our lives. I experienced panic attacks and severe anxiety at times. Money, time, and becoming a new parent was all so overwhelming.

Without having family nearby, it was hard to do anything without another adult guiding us or helping us make smart decisions. Mick's parents passed away before I met him, so he had very little family left. There were some hard days when times were rough. I missed my own family and desperately wanted to create a loving one in my future. I just didn't have the resources to make me feel successful at this yet.

Chapter 13: "You don't have to poop! You're going to have a baby!"

WE DECORATED the baby's room in surfer-baby decor, because Mick 5 and I met in Florida, so we wanted it to be a tropical and happy room. Two walls were painted green and two were painted blue. There were bears on the walls with surfer shorts, palm trees, and surfboards. His mobile was a bunch of suns spinning and wobbling for him to observe and wonder. After searching for the perfect name, we decided to name our son, Matthew. His name means, Gift from God. It is the perfect name for a child that was born from miracles of prayer and patience. I knew he would be my sunshine in such a dark world. I prayed for him and I just knew that my life would not be complete without my son.

Matthew was born in November, that year after thirty-six hours of labor. It was a rough experience, giving birth, but one I will never regret. My bundle of joy was absolutely precious, healthy, and perfect. The thirty-six hours leading up to his first breath were quite difficult. I had early contractions and was given Pitocin to induce labor. I became nauseous and started vomiting. I was unable to give a urine sample, so I had to be hooked up to a catheter. It was all a blur. As the pain increased, I was given an epidural and that helped me rest. I woke up in pain and they checked my contractions. I was given more Pitocin and another epidural over time. I had several different nurses caring for me because I was there for so long. The next thing I knew, I woke up and it was dark in my hospital room. I was in a lot of pain and yelled for the nurse. Mick 5 jumped up around 5:45 in the morning and I told him to get the nurse because I felt like I had to go to the bathroom really bad. The nurse's name was Lisa and I looked at her like she was an angel. She came in the room and I told her that I had to go #2. She would not let me up from the bed. Lisa checked my cervix and said, "You don't have to poop! You're going to have a baby!". WOW!!! Here we go, I pushed and pushed and pushed for twenty minutes and popped the blood vessels under my eyes. Out came a gorgeous baby boy. Our baby boy, Matthew. He was absolutely perfect, even though his head was elongated and he looked a little like an alien when he came out. After the sweet nurses cleaned Matthew up, they wrapped him in a swaddle cloth and handed him to me for the first time. I will never forget this moment. It will stick in my mind forever as the happiest moment

Phillip Pooped in my Pink Patent Leather Purse

of my life. He has blue eyes and blonde hair and the best smile in the world. I could not be more in love with anything else in this world.

Matthew is a miracle. Every child is a miracle. The love I felt towards him is one I never knew existed. I still feel that to this day. I had a purpose, a reason, a sign of hope. I was a mom, finally, and I couldn't have been more elated to have his little seven pound body in my arms. Matthew was taught sign language before the age of 1 to help us communicate without so much frustration. He learned how to ask to be held, tell me "no" or "yes", ask for more, "please", and let me know he is "all done" by nine months old. Speaking followed, along with his love for life. He loved to be read to, danced with, and played with often. Matt loved being pushed on the swings and running around the house with toilet paper. I nursed him for the first year so he was fairly healthy and met his milestones on time. He was my world and our everything.

Mick 5 came home with a purple 27' Baja speed boat one day and surprised us. I was wondering how we were going to pay for such an expense, but it appeared to me as something I was not to worry about. We took the boat out on the water a few times, but not having a home on the water and having to pay for storage during the winter months, I was able to convince my husband to sell it eventually.

This was not the start of our financial troubles. We were broke and the IRS suddenly took everything we had due to other debts owed by my husband at the time. It caused marital grief and hard times, job losses, separation, and too much fighting. I couldn't bear it anymore. I wanted a simpler, more honest life. I went to Bible Study at church and relied on new friends Jane, Evelyn, and women support groups to help me become stronger.

When Matthew was three years old, one day I saw some websites in our computer history that I could not live with, websites that were visited frequently, although not by me. It's hard to explain, but I felt like I had an army of support behind me. I found courage somehow. I had built up strength and hope for a good life. Once I saw what my husband had been searching for online for over a year, I firmly asked Mick to say goodbye to his son and leave the house that was in my name. This was the start of my divorce from my son's dad. I was scared. I had nothing and no one here to really take care of me or help me out. I reached out to a few friends and did my best to count my blessings. I was not working at the time, so I had no income. I had depended on my husband to be sure that bills were paid and we could manage our lifestyle without my income. My teaching certificate renewal required some course work, so I signed up to take classes at Eastern Michigan University. I kicked him out without a plan to pay my bills. My hands were tied financially, because I could not teach or make an income without completing these courses first. It was a very challenging time and I hit rock bottom being completely broke, going through a divorce with a child, and dealing with Mick's anger towards me for the divorce. I had nothing, but a few friends who helped me figure out how to get back on my feet. I had to sell everything I had to eat, and feed my child. It was very humbling, but extremely difficult and lonely.

I lost our family home to the bank and sold our home's furniture for groceries. A friend gave me a personal loan and I found a new place for my son and me to live in Plymouth, MI with a few dollars in my pocket. It was a very cute home to rent in a peaceful neighborhood with flowers growing all around the property. I did not want my son to be raised around the yelling and fighting. We grew apart and I wanted something different. I wanted him to see what a good relationship looked like. I wanted a relationship built on love, honesty, and respect. Why was that so hard to find? I was thirty-seven with a 3-year-old, a few friends, and no family nearby. My mom still lived in Fort Lauderdale, FL and my dad lived in Wisconsin. My brother lived in California with his family, so I was here depending on close friends to get me by in life. I felt alone... a lot! Will I ever catch a break?

I prayed, I cried, I danced, and I made connections to help me cope during this lonely time. I was fairly broke, because I didn't receive a lot of child support and daycare was very expensive. I continued to teach to make a living, but my attitude about life and what had happened to me were pretty shitty. I was negative and struggling to be good at anything. I was cynical and doubted that real love existed. My child was my only hope and even he was struggling during the first few years after my divorce. The divorce affected his behavior. I tried so hard to be positive. It wasn't easy, but once again I got over that bump in the road.

I had held a job since I was fifteen, attempting to pay my bills and manage my life by holding a career that allowed me to be home with my child each summer. I had never thought that not working would ever be an option. I was a working mom with my son. However, he went to school in the same district or school where I taught for many years. We enjoyed our summers together and have many memories of quality mother and son times.

As Matthew became more independent, I started wanting a promising relationship with someone who demonstrated care and protection for my son and me. So I dated and learned some more lessons about loneliness, trust, and patience. I still made time for fun and visited Florida often to see my high school best friends and my mom. A group of ten of us went on a cruise to the Bahamas to celebrate all of us turning forty in 2011 and my best friend, Cindy, was my roommate. We had a blast!

Me and Cindy celebrating our 40th Birthday on a cruise

Phillip Pooped in my Pink Patent Leather Purse

Deja Poo

adj. The feeling of having heard this crap before

Chapter 14: Deja Poo

WHAT'S THE OLD expression, "If you step in shit once, shame on the shit, If you step in it a second time, shame on me". In my twenties, Golfer Brad left me broke and with all of the bills, my first marriage in my thirties left me bankrupt with a darling little boy, so why haven't I learned my lesson?

When my son was seven, I met another man who I eventually married. This was not an ideal relationship and I recently divorced this man. I wanted an honest, real relationship based on unconditional love. I had it once, so I knew it existed. I should have seen the warning signs when we would argue as soon as I brought up topics that made me uncomfortable. He was defensive and could do no wrong. When I set boundaries, I got yelled at and blamed for being the problem. This happened way too often, so I only had so much tolerance for that. I wanted to talk about things we disagreed on and settle them respectfully. That did not happen, so I did not stay married.

I was married to this man for a few weeks when my Dad's girlfriend, Tammy, who lives in Wisconsin, started messaging my husband privately. This went on behind my back and without my knowledge for about 7 months. Tammy broke up with my dad on social media within a few months, a couple of days before Christmas and my Dad's birthday on December 27th. I had my dad drive to Michigan and stay with us for a while to help him get over his broken heart around the holidays. My dad was a wonderful loving grandpa to my son and we called him, Pop Pop.

Matthew and I were happy to have my dad here but we never really saw him smile that year. A few months later, Tammy made her way back into my dad's life on Cinco de Mayo. He sent me a picture of them together drinking margaritas at a Mexican restaurant in Wisconsin. I was shocked to see that my dad was giving her another chance after her immature break up. At this time, my husband confessed that she had been sending him private messages and shared them with me. Tammy was asking my husband why I was such a "bitch" on Thanksgiving and let him know that she wishes she had met someone like him before meeting my dad. She complimented his musical talents and picked up on his charming personality that clearly led her on. There were many other critical comments made to make me look like I was not deserving of his love. He sent the messages to my dad and told him that she is not welcome in our home. No one really stood up for me and told her she was out of line. My feelings didn't matter.

Phillip Pooped in my Pink Patent Leather Purse

A year later, my dad made the choice to marry this woman, despite her interest in my ex-husband. I decided to not attend the wedding, so I have not spoken to my dad since. This has made me very sad to know that my feelings didn't matter and now my dad and I don't speak due to hurt feelings.

I tried to make this marriage work, but I did not want to be yelled at, criticized, or ignored anymore. I wanted a partner, not someone who only cared about making themselves happy. After 4 years of marriage to this man, I went to counseling and sought out professional help and advice. I told my therapist that I have been struggling with feeling happy in my marriage, and I felt very lonely and ignored. After two years of counseling, my therapist told me that my husband is a narcissist and things will never change, so it was divorce or misery. I wasn't prepared to make that change, so it was a shock. I trusted this woman who I spoke to every Saturday at noon for an hour. She seemed to have my best interests in mind, but I still wasn't prepared to end everything. We were together for eight years and I was alone often due to his lifestyle that I did not want. During the last couple of years of this marriage, my second husband would be away from home fourteen to eighteen nights each month working in bars, concerts, or other music venues until late hours. Sometimes he would leave to go out of town for weeks at a time with his band without calling me. I worked full time and raised my son with little influence on his part.

Matthew was not a fan of him either. When I told him that I wanted a separation the first time, he had a temper tantrum for 5 hours, while scaring my son with his verbal outbursts and harsh criticisms. I decided to give him another chance, but after another year, I told him again that I wanted a divorce. I was suddenly the worst person in this world and he tried to turn everyone I knew against me with his lies. I was living another nightmare with this man.

Unfortunately, we were separated but still living together at the time COVID-19 began spreading in the U. S. and people were quarantined in March 2020. My son and I lived upstairs and he lived in the bottom level, so we still had to see him sometimes and know he was in the house.

He would blare his band's music just to make me angry. Due to government order, schools were closed and I worked from home while my son stayed in his bedroom doing online-school for several months. It was a rough divorce because he went after all that I have financially, and I was left broke again. I had been forced to move from the home we bought and be a single mom again. It was freeing to be divorced from him though, because I knew I would not be happy if I had remained married to him. It was hard to think of any reason to stay. I am not all of the names he called me. I am a better person than that. This was a very difficult forgiveness lesson, but I eventually came around after learning about myself and how much I can tolerate. Luckily, I surrounded myself with positive inspiring people who helped me believe that I was worth better. I was miserable and knew I needed to leave.

I learned that actions speak much louder than words. I learned that I need to be heard and listened to, as well as see equal efforts towards a common vision in a relationship. I learned that I am not perfect, but I deserve respect. I learned that I need affection by my loved ones, so I will show it to them. I learned that I want a partner for life in all areas. I learned forgiveness, gratitude, how to meditate, and the importance of being my courageous self because of that relationship. I followed him and his dreams because I did not have the courage to follow my own. Writing this book is my courage, my voice, and my advice for the people who can relate to any of my stories.

I am not giving up hope, as I believe that true love really does exist. You must know who you are and become an observer of yourself. Strive to become what you want in a partner. You must

Phillip Pooped in my Pink Patent Leather Purse

forgive others, all of them, as we are all on our own journey. It only weighs you down if you carry these burdens. But you do not need to continue relationships with everyone you've forgiven.

You have every right to live your life how you see fit. Setting boundaries is healthy.

Phillip may have pooped in my pink patent leather purse, boys looked at my pre-school panties, older men wanted to get me naked and let me know how they felt, but I have remained true to myself and have lived many years forgiving all of this in order to have inner peace. I miss those who passed before me and will forever grieve their loss. I am stronger today than ever and rarely in a bad mood or affected by what life throws in my corner. I'm over the bullshit, and happy to be alive.

> *Everyone you meet is fighting a battle you know nothing about. Be kind. Always.*

Now, I will take you along my journey of how I got my shit together and have created inner peace and unconditional love in my life. I do my best not to step in crap anymore and I am excited to share my experiences that taught me many lessons.

AFTERWORD

I WROTE *Phillip Pooped in my Pink Patent Leather Purse* for several reasons. First and foremost, it felt like a calling for me. I've had the title in my head since I was in my twenties and wanted to write the book, because I already had so many "crappy" things happen to me. At that time, I did not have the strength, love, knowledge, or support to get it done. I have always been an introvert, so I kept my pain inside and didn't share with too many people. Instead, I chose a career path of being a teacher for children who struggle with their emotions, learning, behavior, and mindset. During my twenty-five successful years of teaching students in grades K-12 with learning disabilities and emotional or behavioral special needs in Florida and Michigan, becoming a Boy Mom, trying to be a "good" wife, daughter, friend, etc., then being a single mom to a preschooler, married again, divorced for a second time, raising a teen, etc., I've run into many challenges. I knew that I had to tell my stories and write them all down in one place. My mind doesn't shut off from all of the crazy crap I've lived through. I am constantly questioning why people think they can do what they have done without knowing how it hurt. I have learned a lot about forgiveness, and I realize that we are all making mistakes and hurting others in the meantime. I have been intruded upon and treated like poo on a shoe and I don't know how much more I can take. I've been diagnosed with forms of anxiety, depression, and PTSD and have spent years in counseling to overcome them all. I'm so blessed to be here today to share my true stories with you. I have experienced a lot of pain and found it hard to focus on anything, but writing this book has been healing for me. I meditate before each writing session to help me go back in time and feel these raw emotions once again. Releasing built-up feelings is powerful, and I highly recommend it to anyone who can relate to any of my experiences or who has painful ones that have changed their path as well.

> IT TOOK ME QUITE A LONG TIME TO DEVELOP A VOICE AND NOW THAT I HAVE IT, I'M NOT GOING TO BE SILENT.
>
> -Madeleine Albright

Secondly, I want to help people understand that children NEED to be listened to and not ignored. Your child will be an adult one day and needs to know how to cope with life's challenges. Don't have children if you don't want to commit a large part of your time, thoughts, energy, and money in order to raise good, healthy people. Read books and educate yourself. It doesn't help to yell, scold, or criticize either. Oh, and by the way, acting-in-silence is louder than you think. Don't avoid the hard work. Don't ignore the child who spends too much time by themselves. Ask, Listen, Lead, and Guide your children lovingly as you would want someone to do with you. Children who grow up with emotional neglect suffer deeply as adults, but they also often hide it from the world and feel very alone in their struggle as a result. Empower your children with the tools they need to be strong but kind people. Be there to listen and empathize. Children do not have the tools or ability to just "suck it up and be a man" when they are young.

Young ladies are not "ridiculous" or "drama queens". They need strategies and someone to listen to what they think is real.

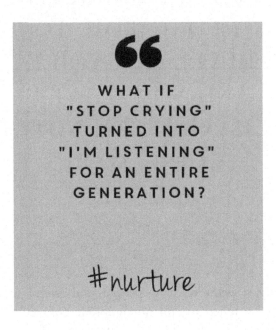

A wise woman and good friend, Jane, once told me something that made me realize this. For many years, I was a single mom, and took that role very seriously because I only had one child. He is my biggest blessing on this planet and I am so grateful for being his MOM. There were some really difficult times being a single mom. I had some lonely, dark, tearful, hard, and penniless days where I would lose hope and feel a heavy heart when I was a single mom. It was even harder when my son spent time with his dad when he was younger. One day, I told Jane my struggles with patience, disciplining, and the tough parts about raising my son during some challenging years. I remember confessing, "Being a parent is very difficult", but she corrected me. Jane profoundly stated, "Most people can be a parent. Being a good parent is very difficult." I care more about being a good parent than I do about anything else at

Phillip Pooped in my Pink Patent Leather Purse

this point in my life. My son's love woke me up and changed me. I suddenly felt responsible for how someone perceives this world, and I have committed to self-healing, self-advocacy, self-love, and having the courage to speak my truth. I have made raising him a priority, because I appreciate him so much. He's my little gift from GOD. I chose my career as a teacher because I appreciated having my parents around all summer spending quality time with us. I wanted to be available for my son and I've always been good with kids, because I have a strong empathetic side. I have an ability to understand their emotions and difficulties. I've never loved anyone or anything more than my son. I never knew this kind of love ever existed. It's quite magical, because I prayed for him and it took me over two years to conceive this blessing. He has been my sunshine during these past fifteen years! Being a Mom has helped me become a better teacher and better human as well.

My mom and me

Another reason I wrote, PPIMPPLP, is because I strongly believe that… woman should never be afraid to say "NO". Our voice should be heard, especially without worrying about a man that might get angry and hurt us. Boys and men…we need you to validate our feelings and hear our cries. I want men to realize that females are so much more than a physical body that they think can be used like a toy or be shown off like a trophy. I understand that you are these sexual beings, but having self-control shows strength and earns respect. It bothers me that some girls and women try so hard to dress sexy to get a man's attention and that our society encourages this in all forms, causing women to have eating disorders, depression, anxiety, body dysmorphia, etc.

Ladies of all ages, cover up your cleavage and your ass cheeks. Stop enticing the perverts, rapists, pedophiles, and kidnappers in this world. They crave more. They have pictures of you on their phones. You know what happens next. GROSS! They are in their room or car taking care of business. But it happens all the time. Every second of every day. You can still be beautiful and feminine, but not show so much skin. Ladies, respect yourself, please! Some of us don't want the attention, gawking, the disrespectful body scan, the unwanted notes revealing your infatuation for my body or your desire to have sex with me, the head-turns, and the cheating or gawking husbands who pretend to do no wrong. Know your worth, dear women.

My son Matthew and me

In addition, I highly encourage you to educate yourself and go after your dreams. Clear your mind. Meditate. Make sure you do what makes you happy. Think about what you want. Reach out to people who can help you accomplish goals and dreams by networking. Make yourself feel extremely proud. Don't give up! My investment in my degree and education has been my saving grace. It continues to feed my soul. Knowledge is power and ignorance is bliss. Be prepared. Be a good person and help others in need. Beauty is intrinsically edifying. If we all do it, then some of us no longer suffer. Stand together. Be brave. Be smart. Be more

Phillip Pooped in my Pink Patent Leather Purse

than just a pretty face. Don't be degraded or settle for anything less than real blind love. If this even exists.

> Being pretty won't keep a man, sex won't keep a man, A baby won't keep a man. Heck being a good woman barely keeps a man. The only thing that'll keep a man is a **man that wants to be kept.**

Next, I want to show the importance of empathy in our world, even for people who smile every day and show up giving it their all. I get teased for trying to be a "life-changer" or I hear other gossipy words from people who don't understand my perspective. I have committed my life to researching and reading hundreds of books, articles, and community forums about how to become my best self, understand my brain and emotions, cope with anxiety, depression, PTSD, childhood emotional neglect, abuse, emotional rape, learning disabilities, ADHD, autism, LGBT life, eating disorders, living with a narcissist, or anything else that can make life difficult. I know what it feels like to experience many of them, as you have read in PPIMPPLP. It makes me feel good to help people who struggle with life, because I am still on this journey. We need each other! People like to talk to me about their problems and I like listening. This book is my way of opening up and telling everyone about my struggles. I hope you will show compassion towards me, as I have done to others.

> I admire people
> who choose
> to shine
> even after
> all the storms
> they've been through.

Lastly, I wrote this book to show how important it is to forgive others and yourself. I believe that everyone is struggling with something. I love my parents very much, but they weren't the perfect parents that I expected, because they came from heartbreaking homes as well. My asthmatic dad was raised by his overprotective, frugal mother because his father was an abusive alcoholic and was raised during the Great Depression. I don't think he had a very good role model for a father. My mother struggled socially as a child and finally came out of the closet as a lesbian in

2000, after being married to my Dad for thirty-three years. None of us had a clue. She was dealing with her own secrets and demons, so it was probably difficult for her to see mine or help me cope when I was struggling. I believe that we are all trying to be something. Many of us are trying our best with what we are given. FORGIVE people. Some need encouragement and inspiration. Some need an eye opening experience. Many people need to read my book!

When we show compassion and empathy for others, it helps people know that they are loved unconditionally. I hope you will try to place less blame on what people have done to you and see them as growing humans, like us all. No one is perfect and that's what makes us all unique. But most importantly, I hope you find your voice. I hope you learn to love yourself, to forgive yourself—even with all of your own flaws. I hope you learn to be your own best friend and talk kindly to yourself. Be kind, patient, and loving towards your inner child as if you were your own amazing mother. The more we understand, the more we can forgive. Love is the answer. It starts with YOU!

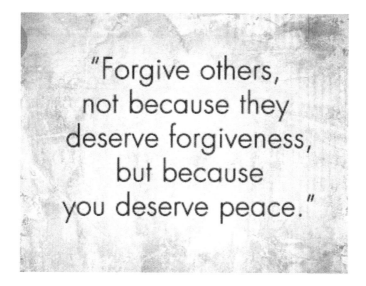

POSITIVE THOUGHTS

Life has taught me I am not always in control. Life is full of experiences, lessons, heartbreak and pain. But, it has also shown me love, beauty, possibility and new beginnings. Embrace it all. It makes us who we are, and after ever storm comes a clear sky.

Epilogue

AFTER READING MY memoir, you may think that I had some pretty shitty experiences. For many years I dwelled on every negative situation I was in, and I had a very difficult time finding hope and joy during certain phases. Yet as I am about to turn fifty in a few months while writing this, I am actually grateful to have all of these past experiences - good and bad. Without them, I would have never learned self-love, self-compassion, and self-forgiveness. I had to learn how to become my own best friend - a positive voice in my head. I simply did for myself what I would do for my son, for my friends, for my students, for my family, and for anyone else I love. I speak to myself now with kindness, gentleness, and respect. I have a firm belief that I am not only a survivor, but also a strong woman with good morals and values. I want the best for people and I've had to let go of some throughout my life because we just weren't vibing along our respective journeys. Others have let go of me for the same reason, and I'm okay with that. I learned that forgiveness is not only for those who are forgiven, but also for those who forgive. I suddenly feel a great load off of my shoulders and I feel more inner peace. I choose not to walk around with regrets - only lessons. I pay attention more. I woke up. I am aware and content and do my best to live in the moment.

For my job, I've been trained in Integrated Thematic Instruction, Brain Gym, Multiple Intelligences, Whole Brain learning, Mindfulness, and several other areas that are brain-behavior-focused. This led me to become interested in meditation and this has worked wonders for me to live in the moment and breathe. I went to therapy for personal counseling twice in my life. The first time from the ages of 22-26, and again from 45-48. If anyone experiences anything I've been through, then I recommend counseling. If you have a good connection with your person, then it's like hanging out with an expensive best friend who is also very smart. I have learned so much from my therapists and working in my profession as a special education teacher for the past twenty-five years. Patience, tolerance, and compassion are necessary when working with individuals who don't fit the mold in our society. I knew that I required a little extra attention when I was younger and I was happy to work on cases with children and teens who could benefit from what I've learned.

Two practices that have helped me a lot are feeling gratitude daily and recognizing the abundance in our lives and on our beautiful planet. Each day I now wake up and feel grateful for my morning cup of coffee, and then focus on a few more things that I'm grateful for on that particular day. Maybe a boring meeting got cancelled or I'm looking forward to wearing a new outfit. Sometimes, I even think about what I'm going to have for dinner that night and I feel excited if it's tacos or something else that I love. These are just my ideas. I almost always include my loved ones such as my son, partner, family, friends, and pets each day.

Paying attention to our plentiful earth, I see so many trees, branches, leaves, pieces of soil, rays of sunshine, sand, snow, clouds, water, molecules, atoms, cells, and stars. I can't help but wonder if there is a better life out there. It brings me hope every day. We live in such a big world and I hope to explore it. I decided to create a better life for myself. I decided to be happy almost every day. It is a choice for me, but it has become addictive. I am always learning about our world and remain curious about people and places all over our planet. When I was a little girl, we had a set of encyclopedias in our home. My mom would sit me on her lap and say, "Where do you want to go today?". I'd name a place, like Hawaii, Africa, or Greece and she would find the section in the encyclopedia that showed me all about this area. My mom would read to me as I looked at the pictures. I learned about - and respected - many cultures across our globe. I was amazed at how differently people live all over this planet. It allowed me to see that my life isn't so terrible and that there is someone out there who has it worse than me. It helped me take away my self-pity when I was down about life and this increased my gratitude for all things present.

I've learned how to have enough courage to say "No" or "Goodbye" when I am being asked to do something against my will. It takes an enormous amount of courage to live an authentic life, to follow your path, and to choose not to care what anyone else thinks of you or how you are living your life. I feel the responsibility to be a role model for my son and show him that people will treat you how you allow them to treat you. I stand up for myself and have gained a voice. I have realized my worth by watching others who inspire me. People show courage in different ways, but being brave is really about being true to yourself. This is why I dedicated this book to my mom. It took my mom over 50 years to find the courage to become her true self and live her own authentic life with her partner. Coming out of the closet as a lesbian principal in Miami was a shock to many. I had a very difficult time with this because my mom was a new person to me. I had to get to know my mom all over again and see her as the person that she desired to be, not just as the mother to my brother and me. Practicing unconditional love and acceptance remains a challenge that is worth more than gold.

Most importantly, I learned how to forgive myself and be kind to myself. I've made a lot of mistakes in my first fifty years, I've given too many chances to many, and I hope that

I'm done getting my purse pooped in. My dad always told me that people who have a hard beginning usually have a better ending. I pray, listen, and seek love and forgiveness. Stop believing you are a victim to life. Life is about self-perception. I stop and wonder if all of the crap in my life happened because I expected the worst to happen each time. It was all I knew. It was hard for me to draw water from my dry well. I had little resources left at times and lacked hope for a good future. I am learning to believe that I am deserving of good things in my life. I remember the men who did not raise their voice at me during an argument or disagreement. I remember the ones who did. I had to learn to forgive myself for allowing them to hurt me. But I feel it in my chest when I am yelled at. It's a burning flame of anxiety and fear. My heart beats to the point of exhaustion when this happens now. I have learned that I should not be afraid. When I feel fear, I am drawing it to myself. Walk away calmly and talk later. I believe in love. I believe in myself. I believe that there is good in this world, but I must open my eyes to all of the choices I have made.

I hope you enjoyed my first memoir. I have plans for two more coming soon. My next book will be about the amazing experiences I've had that are exciting and positive, not shitty. These are what kept me alive. These are stories of my blessings and people who inspired me! After that, I will share my stories of being a special education teacher for 25 years in K-12 grades. You don't want to miss them. I have just as many stories about those two topics and I promise you'll love them if you liked this memoir. Please follow me on Instagram: @wendyzellauthor. I am a new author, so if you liked or even loved my book, please tell a friend or even fifty. Thank you and I wish you a beautiful life filled with love, peace, and courage.

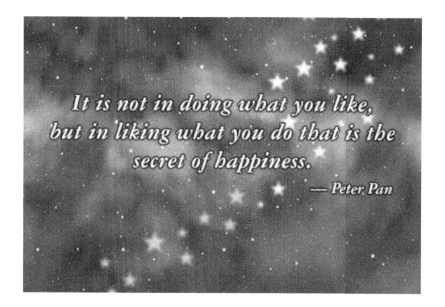

Acknowledgements

THERE ARE some very special people I'd like to acknowledge, and without them, I would not have been able to make this dream of mine come true.

To begin, I am forever grateful for all of the teachers I had when I was in school, and all of the teachers I was lucky enough to work with in grades K-12 these past 26 years. They all deserve a shout-out. I learned so much from other teachers on how to write with my heart. I had the honor of co-teaching with some amazing educators.

Thank you to ALL of my family, friends, students, and co-workers who have been listening to my stories for years and hearing me say that I'm going to write a book someday. I finally did it!

Once, I received a big coffee mug as a gift from a student, Aliyah, with a message on the front that read: "Write Your Own Story," and then it all began. I started writing the poop stories and couldn't stop.

Special thanks go to my talented and artistic brother, John Zell. Your unicorn is one of a kind, just like you. I love you Big Brother and your awesome family in California! If I didn't have the daily support and encouragement of Patricia Zell, Matthew, and

Christopher Howell, this would not be possible. They all kept me going and understood my commitment to this book. Thank you all for believing in me and being there to help, especially during these final days when it felt like I would never be finished with editing.

Chris, you have been a true partner and I am forever grateful for your taking this journey with me. Thank you also to your beautiful and talented daughter, McKenna Genovese, for your time and our photography session. I am so grateful and love you both!

The Howell Family has been so kind and encouraging to help me make this dream become a reality.

I have many close friends who encouraged me, laughed at my stories, and kept me sane these past few years while writing this book. I am especially grateful for the friendship of My Florida Girls, My Michigan friends, the Bs, and Teacher Mondays in the summer. I can't wait to write about many of you compassionate and loving women in my next memoir, Say Something Sunshine.

Special thanks to my editor, Matt Cubberly, for making me feel FANTASTIC about my memoir and for your excellent editing work.

A special word of gratitude is due to Rodney—The Man—Miles, my book's beauty maker and designer. Rodney took my vision and created this masterpiece of a memoir. You have been so helpful every step of the way, Rodney. I knew that being a fellow Gator, your efforts would not fail. I would have never made it to publishing without you.

Finally, I would like to acknowledge with gratitude the support of my readers. Your encouraging comments make me want to keep writing. Thank you.

About the Author

WENDY ZELL is a writer and author of a new memoir titled *Phillip Pooped In My Pink Patent Leather Purse: A Memoir of Adversity, Courage, & Self Love*. It's been more than four decades since five-year-old Phillip purposefully went "number two" in little Wendy's favorite pink purse. An incident like that would stink for any toddler (no pun intended). However, for Wendy the episode was a symbolic representation of all the crap she's had to endure in this crazy little thing we call life.

Wendy was born and raised in south Florida but later relocated to Michigan. She has a K-12 Special Education teaching degree from the University of Florida (Go Gators!) and has been a special education teacher for the past twenty six years. She continued her education at Eastern Michigan University where she took courses such as Children's Literacy, Native American Literature, Leadership, and Mindfulness. An educator to her core, helping others is her true purpose. It's also why she became an author.

Wendy's greatest accomplishment in life is her 16-year-old son Matthew.

During her free time she enjoys writing, home decorating and improvement projects, traveling, hiking, dancing, and of course spending time with family and friends. She enjoys weekend adventures with her caring and fun-loving boyfriend, Christopher. Walks on beaches or nature trailing are just as common as karaoke parties for two in their living room. She continues to teach high school students in her local neighborhood and enjoys tutoring young children how to read and write.

I always love to hear from my readers!

Drop me a note, feedback, or ask a question!

And thanks for reading!

Web: www.WendyZell.com
Facebook: www.facebook.com/ppimpplp
Instagram: @wendyzellauthor/
Email: wendyazell@gmail.com

Made in the USA
Monee, IL
10 August 2021